estherpress

Books for Courageous Women

ESTHER PRESS VISION

Publishing diverse voices that encourage and equip women to walk courageously in the light of God's truth for such a time as this.

BIBLICAL STATEMENT OF PURPOSE

"For if you keep silent at this time, relief and deliverance will rise for the Jews from another place, but you and your father's house will perish. And who knows whether you have not come to the kingdom for such a time as this?"

Esther 4:14 (ESV)

What people are saying about …

purpose doesn't pause

"I have always loved books that feel like coffee with a friend, and this is exactly that. Purpose can be found in every single season God has placed you in; there is never a season that is wasted and this book serves as a beautiful reminder of that. If you are in a season where you are struggling to see your purpose, then these words are for you."

Sadie Robertson Huff, author, speaker, and founder of Live Original

"If you're feeling stuck or like your life has been put on pause, this is the book you need. Hope's healing words rooted in God's Word will create a safe haven for you as you find a way through the uncertainty into a transformation you never thought possible. I loved the inspiring stories and the community of women who shaped this beautiful and helpful book. Read it with your friends and show up to your purpose together, no matter what today looks like!"

Lysa TerKeurst, #1 *New York Times* bestselling author and president of Proverbs 31 Ministries

"*Purpose Doesn't Pause* is a beautiful reminder that no matter what happens in life, God has put us on a mission to represent Him and enjoy Him!"

Tori Hope Petersen, bestselling author of *Fostered*

"Are you feeling stuck or confused about your purpose? Then this book is for you! Through personal stories, biblical examples, and insightful interviews, Hope beautifully guides us through what's holding us back so we can walk free and full of purpose!"

Nicole Jacobsmeyer, speaker and
author of *Take Back Your Joy*

"*Purpose Doesn't Pause* is like one of those much-needed refreshing chats with a friend where you leave encouraged and empowered. Hope sweetly but firmly builds her readers up in God's plans for them. Hope's must-read encouragement helps you move from just watching others live out their purpose to finding freedom and excitement to live out your God-given purpose. This is a book you need on your nightstand and one you'll want to read through over and over again."

Megan Edmonds, *She Lives*
Purposefully podcast host

"*Purpose Doesn't Pause* is just what you need. Hope does a fantastic job reminding you that God has designed you for exactly what He's called you. If you are walking through a waiting season, or a season of uncertainty—this is a gentle reminder that God is in your corner and you've been designed to fulfill your purpose! Thank you, Hope—for being such a faithful steward and friend of Jesus. We are blessed because of you!"

Alison Delamota, *My Morning*
Devotional podcast host

"This book is a powerful read for anyone feeling stuck and provides practical tools to combat confusion and walk boldly in your calling. I wish I had this in my twenties!"

Nicole Renard, Instagram, TikTok, and YouTube content creator

"In her book *Purpose Doesn't Pause,* Hope Reagan Harris offers solid biblical teachings and writes for every weary, confused, and wandering heart that longs to find God's purpose for their lives. Like a friend, Hope creates space for honest conversation and offers her reader opportunities for reflection. Hope courageously invites us into her story and tenderly points us to the God-given purpose within our own lives."

Cassandra Speer, bestselling author, Bible teacher, and vice president of Her True Worth

"You are not alone in your confusing season of life, and Hope knows how to bring a support group of Christian women into your living room to remind you of that. This book makes you feel like you spent a day with your best friend. Hope's rich wisdom and insight will calm your anxious thoughts and worried heart and remind you of the truth. Through relatable life stories, songs, and reflective questions, she will guide you out of confusion and decision fatigue into clear thinking grounded in God's Word."

Mikella Van Dyke, founder of Chasing Sacred

purpose doesn't pause

purpose doesn't pause

Finding Freedom From What's Holding You Back

hope reagan harris

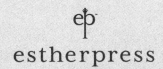

esther press

Books for Courageous Women
from David C Cook

PURPOSE DOESN'T PAUSE
Published by Esther Press
An imprint of David C Cook
4050 Lee Vance Drive
Colorado Springs, CO 80918 U.S.A.

Integrity Music Limited, a Division of David C Cook
Brighton, East Sussex BN1 2RE, England

The EP graphic logo is a trademark of Esther Press.

The website addresses recommended throughout this book are offered as a
resource to you. These websites are not intended in any way to be or imply an
endorsement on the part of David C Cook, nor do we vouch for their content.

Unless otherwise noted, all Scripture quotations are taken from the Holy Bible, New
International Version®, NIV®. Copyright © 1973, 2011 by Biblica, Inc.™ Used by
permission of Zondervan. All rights reserved worldwide. www.zondervan.com. The
"NIV" and "New International Version" are trademarks registered in the United
States Patent and Trademark Office by Biblica, Inc.™ Scripture quotations marked
ESV are taken from the ESV® Bible (The Holy Bible, English Standard Version®),
copyright © 2001 by Crossway, a publishing ministry of Good News Publishers.
Used by permission. All rights reserved. Scripture quotations marked MSG are taken
from THE MESSAGE, copyright © 1993, 2018 by Eugene H. Peterson. Used by
permission of NavPress, represented by Tyndale House Publishers. All rights reserved.

Library of Congress Control Number 2023935152
ISBN 978-0-8307-8586-5
eISBN 978-0-8307-8604-6

Published in association with Books and Such Literary Management, 2222
Cleveland Ave. #1005, Santa Rosa, CA 95403, www.booksandsuch.com.

The Team: Susan McPherson, Julie Cantrell,
James Hershberger, Jack Campbell, Karen Sherry
Cover Design: Micah Kandros

Printed in the United States of America
First Edition 2023

1 2 3 4 5 6 7 8 9 10

060923

*To Will – Thank you for walking
with me through the highs and the lows.
Getting to do life with you is
the greatest blessing. You'll never
know what you mean to me.*

*To Remi – Writing this book while
you were growing in my belly was
the sweetest gift. I pray that you
walk with Jesus all of your
days and shine His bright light
wherever He takes you.*

contents

foreword

I met Hope when we were both writers for Live Original and immediately knew we would become good friends. We were brushing our teeth in a cabin in the middle of the woods of Louisiana, and we just connected as we talked openly about life, Jesus, and changes.

Hope has a gentle spirit and can make everyone around her feel welcomed and wanted. She doesn't claim perfection, she lives out joy, and she leads well. Also, she is the cutest mama and the most energetic friend, and she will drive hours to see you for ten minutes—but that's not the point. I could talk hours about the character and love Hope lives out, but honestly, after you read this book, I think you'll be able to see her heart and character in one chapter.

Hope is gracious and gentle. She's a talented writer but, more importantly, a humble and loyal friend. The best part about Hope is, in her writing, she is always willing to go first and share the hard (when most wouldn't go there first). She relates her pain, change, and difficult experience to her readers. She truly becomes their friend. And I truly believe this book is some of the best work I've seen for this generation.

Purpose can sound daunting, confusing, and overwhelming. But Hope makes it understandable, exciting, and tangible—even when you're in your twenties, teens, disappointed, busy, or in the in-between. Sometimes I read Christian books and struggle to connect with the authors. This book is different and genuinely a needed anthem for a generation struggling with control, the unknown, comparison, and finding meaning in the everyday.

I can look at my life and sometimes feel bummed it isn't what I pictured. This book isn't just something I can recommend; it's something I needed.

Through Hope's stories and words you'll experience the peace I felt as I turned the pages and realized that even though life isn't how I pictured, it is so much better. Through her words I realized my closed doors were a blessing because they were God giving me clarity, not disappointment. Her words were a hug as well as the motivation and discernment I needed to power through in my current season, even though life isn't going how I want.

Chances are you too picked up this book because you're in a similar season as I am. Life isn't what you expected—or even more frustrating, you don't even know what to expect. This book is a push and gentle reminder of the joy we experience in the unknown, the twists and the turns.

I recommend Hope as a friend, as a mentor, and as a writer. I hope you too get the joy of brushing your teeth next to her kind and gentle spirit, preferably in the woods in freezing temperatures.

But if you never get that experience, reading *Purpose Doesn't Pause* is what you need to experience her wisdom, giftings, kindness, and friendship. This book is an answered prayer for me and, I believe, for many in my generation.

Grace Valentine
Speaker
Author of *Am I Enough?*, *What Will They Think?*,
Is It Just Me?, and *To the Girl Looking for More*

chapter 1 — what if we aren't stuck?

"Here is the only thing that will ever get us there."[1]

Christine Caine

Have you ever experienced a season of paralyzing confusion? A moment in life when you just feel *stuck* and don't know what to do next? Maybe you're going through a gut-wrenching breakup, an unexpected loss, or a mistake that feels unforgivable. Or perhaps this time of uncertainty roots from an unexpected rejection, something good coming to an end, or nothing going as planned.

The list of possible reasons you've picked up this book goes on and on. But the bottom line is that confusion can get the best of all of us. Regardless of what brings us here today, I'm betting we've all at one time or another (or maybe all the time!) found ourselves feeling numb to the things we used to enjoy, full of anxiety about what steps to take next, and so exhausted that we don't know how to purposefully show up anymore.

Isn't it crazy how easily this feeling of defeat can sneak into our lives? That's exactly how confusion greeted me.

I'd spent five years after college building a successful career in the corporate world, and all had been going well. I'd happily worked for one employer and had never experienced anything like the frustrations that came when I accepted a new position within that same company.

Red flags started popping up the first week in that new role, and as time went on, the flags only got bigger and brighter (think maraschino cherries). By week three, I learned my new team hadn't been including me in meetings because they were unsure of my role. No wonder my calendar had remained so clear!

This is when confusion set in. My boss had clearly defined my role to the team numerous times, so their excuses weren't adding up. Did they want me to fail? Were they all against me? Why was this happening?

Another month of being excluded was painful enough, but then a senior leader confronted me with a particularly hurtful comment: "Why were you hired for this role?" He went on to tell me that he didn't think my skill set matched their needs and that he wasn't sure how to use me on their project.

As you can imagine, my confidence level reached an all-time low and my confusion level continued to rise.

For months I felt rejected, unvalued, and lonely. My world as I knew it was falling apart. Day after day, I found myself wishing I could return to my previous position. Accepting this new role was supposed to be a move up in the world. It wasn't supposed to make me feel defeated and burned out.

It was taking everything in me not to quit.

a random, life-changing bike ride

As crazy as it sounds, a Peloton ride changed my perspective. One night, out of stress and frustration from yet another bad day at work, I hopped on my dusty Peloton exercise bike to take a spin and de-stress. The video class had already started when my husband, Will, walked in to find that I was just sitting there on the bike, watching the class play out on the screen.

He laughed and said, "Hope, you have to move your legs."

We both cracked up. I knew he was right, but I was so mentally exhausted that mustering up the energy to move my legs was no small feat.

There had to be another way to ride out this confusion, right? What was I missing here?

Here's what happened after laughing over my "exercise" routine. I stopped being an observer of the class, I turned up the resistance on the bike, and I gave it my all like my Peloton instructor was telling me to do. As my posture went from defeated to determined, I was finally ready to take on the challenge coming my way.

That's when an aha moment hit me. How Will had found me sitting on my bike was exactly how I had been sitting in my life. Confused, exhausted, defeated ... *stuck*!

Just like in the spin class, I had become a bystander observing life going on around me. Instead of showing up at my job and giving it my all to work through the challenges, I had been letting the resistance stifle me.

That's when I realized I could make a different choice. I could choose to fully show up and combat the challenges facing me at work. And in life.

What might happen if we all dared to shift perspective? What if this season of confusion could transform us in ways we can't yet imagine? What if this season is challenging us to show up fully to the life God has given us?

What if, instead of being observers, we choose to live every day as if our PURPOSE DOESN'T PAUSE?

You and I are going to share this season together, but we aren't going to sit still and watch other people live out their purpose. And we aren't going to end this journey in the same way we start. Instead, we're going to shift our posture from defeated to determined. We're going to get unstuck. We're going to show up and live our true purpose, just as God has called us to do. Because life is short, and God doesn't press pause.

the problem with confusion

The week after my Peloton awakening, I arrived at work with a new attitude. I was finally ready to do whatever it took to turn my story around.

Fortuitously, a Zoom meeting was already on the calendar, so I decided to take that opportunity to share my concerns with a trusted mentor. Before I could finish the story, he looked at me and said, "You aren't stuck, Hope. You just think you are."

Maybe my mentor was on to something.

After spending some time with Google, I realized I wasn't the only one who had experienced this "stuck" feeling. I also learned that we tend to respond to uncertainty by "spontaneously generating plausible explanations."[2]

In other words, what if my mentor was right not just about me but also about you? Maybe we aren't really *stuck* at all. Maybe we just think we are.

With this new knowledge, I started to believe that God had put me in that position on purpose, for a purpose. I chose to believe that He was preparing me for what He would be calling me to step into next.

Perhaps if I tried to bypass this difficult experience, I would miss out on something God was planning to use for His good and His glory.

Coming to this belief was not short on pain or suffering. For months, online job searches had become my hobby. I applied for job after job only to be greeted daily with the automated message: "Don't be discouraged, but we're going with someone else."

I cried out to God, "If You want me here, I'll stay. Close any door that isn't supposed to be opened."

Sure enough, every possible door slammed in my face. But then I realized that nothing else was working out because He had placed me there intentionally. And He was using this frustrating experience to do some important work in my heart.

Eventually my husband and in-laws encouraged me to tell my boss how the tension at work was impacting not just my job performance but also my overall well-being.

After a lot of prayer, I went for it. My boss's response blew me away. She told me that she had been in a similar place at one point in her career, and she wanted to be there for me like she wished someone had been there for her. She offered to change up my responsibilities, and she encouraged me to have a conversation with the senior leader who was constantly questioning me.

Before I had the painful conversation with him, I again asked God to be with me. The stomach butterflies leading up to that conversation were supersized. I don't know if I've ever felt so nervous. When we finally connected, he apologized. He told me what he valued about my skill set and said he wished I had talked to him about my concerns earlier.

For the first time in a long time, I felt free. I still was confused about why this was happening to me, but I started to see that my mentor had been right all along. I wasn't stuck. I'd just thought I was.

What if the same is true for you?

when problems take us by surprise

Most of us spend far too much time trying to understand why a painful experience is happening to us.

One evening after work, I sat down on the cozy gray couch in my living room and opened my Bible to 1 Peter 4–5. Have you ever read a certain verse and felt as if God was speaking directly to you?

Before you read these verses, it's important to understand the context behind the book of 1 Peter. As one of Jesus' first disciples, Peter wrote this letter to encourage Christians who were being persecuted in brutal ways. He reminded them that suffering is a part of Christian life but that God would strengthen them, and glory would come through their hope in Christ.

Let's look at a few verses that stood out as I read these two chapters in 1 Peter:

- "Dear friends, do not be surprised at the fiery ordeal that has come on you to test you, as though something strange were happening to you. But rejoice inasmuch as you participate in the sufferings of Christ, so that you may be overjoyed when his glory is revealed" (1 Peter 4:12–13).

- "Humble yourselves, therefore, under God's mighty hand, that he may lift you up in due time. Cast all your anxiety on him because he cares for you" (1 Peter 5:6–7).

- "Be alert and of sober mind. Your enemy the devil prowls around like a roaring lion looking for someone to devour. Resist him, standing firm in the faith, because you know that the family of believers throughout the world is undergoing the same kind of sufferings" (1 Peter 5:8–9).

- "And the God of all grace, who called you to his eternal glory in Christ, after you have suffered a little while, will himself restore you and make you strong, firm and steadfast" (1 Peter 5:10).

I love how Peter's message still speaks truth to us today. He tells us **not to be surprised** when sufferings hit us and explains that this is the unfortunate reality of the world we live in. We are called to live a life that looks more and more like Jesus' every day, so why are we surprised when hard things happen to us?

We don't have to be surprised because we are equipped with faith. We don't have to fear because God is FOR us, and He will make us "strong, firm and steadfast" through our troubles (1 Peter 5:10). And we don't have to feel alone in our suffering because believers around the world are suffering along with us. We are all going through this together.

This is why it's so important to lean not on our own truth, but to lean on the Living Word—the one and only truth. As we rely on God's Word, we become equipped to step into the abundant life He created for us, showing up fully to face whatever situations He brings us to today.

See? No matter the challenge, with God on our side, we really do have everything we need to face any situation in our lives right now.

Romans 8:18 says, "For I consider that the sufferings of this present time are not worth comparing with the glory that is to be revealed to us" (ESV). Jesus has already conquered death and made a way for us to spend eternity with Him. He has already given us a path to victory, so let's start living like it.

Looking back, I now see just how far God has carried me. While I was stressing over little details at work, He pointed me to a verse that made me see that things weren't really as complicated as I'd somehow believed.

> **A**s we rely on God's Word, we become equipped to step into the abundant life He created for us, showing up fully to face whatever situations He brings us to today.

Matthew 22:37–39 says best what God calls us to do: "Jesus replied: 'Love the Lord your God with all your heart and with all your soul and with all your mind.' This is the first and greatest commandment. And the second is like it: 'Love your neighbor as yourself.'"

Isn't that simple? It took questioning my situation at work to understand the real role we are called to play in our everyday lives—love God and love people.

Want to know the best news? We don't have to live this out alone. Matthew 28:18–20 reads, "And Jesus came and said to them, 'All authority in heaven and on earth has been given to me. Go therefore and make disciples of all nations, baptizing them in the name of the Father and of the Son and of the Holy Spirit, teaching them to observe all that I have commanded you. And behold, I am with you always, to the end of the age'" (ESV).

what's next?

Since we'll need to pivot from a posture of defeat to one of determination, why not do so together? Each chapter in *Purpose Doesn't Pause* will focus on a specific experience in our everyday lives that can leave us feeling confused and stuck. Together, we'll uncover God's truth so we can show up and fully live our purpose—to love God and love others.

After each chapter, we'll engage in a purposeful chat with a twentysomething woman who has struggled with challenges similar to ours.

This book is designed to be a community-focused experience. The ultimate hope is that it won't be a one-and-done read but something we refer to throughout our daily lives. The more dog-eared pages, underlines, and notes in the margins … the better!

We all know how confusion can leave us feeling, so don't feel pressured to read this book in any specific order. It's designed so you can turn to any chapter that resonates with you today and trust that the rest will be waiting for you when the time comes.

To bring this full circle, let's go back to the Peloton story. Picture this:

The bike symbolizes the journey God has given us.

 The seat symbolizes where God has us right now.
 The handlebars symbolize God's truth because
that is where we put all our weight as we show
up for the purposeful ride that God intentionally
placed us on.

The screen showing the instructor teaching the
class can symbolize how we will focus our eyes
on Jesus, starting now.

What a picture. It's time to live out our purpose. Are you ready? Let's do this!

chapter 2 when we're questioning why we are where we are

"Don't worry about finding your purpose. If you are seeking after God, your purpose will find you."[1]

Tony Evans

What if God is both using us and preparing us right now? What if we don't have to search for our purpose because it is already available wherever we are? What if this seat is exactly where we are supposed to be sitting?

These are the issues we'll begin exploring in this chapter, as we work together to:

- ponder our questions and reflect

- take a closer look at the life of someone in the Bible who had every reason to question why God placed him where he was
- pivot our heart posture so we can begin living our purpose in the here and now

Sound like a plan?

Before we dive in, I wish we could watch a video of me from 2017 as I walked into my first day of work at a tech company in Arlington, Virginia. Will and I had gotten engaged the last semester of our senior year of college, and after graduation, I just needed a job—any paying job.

This wasn't the recruiter's first rodeo. She must have known exactly what to say to get any fresh grad to accept the job offer, so she told me I'd be managing and serving the executive members on a dozen highly important Fortune 500 accounts.

It sounded right up my alley—building relationships and offering customer service. However, the first day looked much different than I'd pictured. If we could see that video today, we'd be cracking up at my facial expression as my boss led me to my desk and … to my new *headset*.

Turns out, each week I was expected to make 250 phone calls, send 150 emails, and leave 50 voice mails, with a goal of getting as many executives as possible to sign up for retreats the company was hosting.

It quickly became clear that this was pretty much a call-center job.

Guess what made this season even more humbling? Before we were allowed to recruit members to come to the executive retreats, we had to pass a call test with our manager. Out of 75 people in my start class that July, I was the only one who failed!

Our stories may be different, but how often do we find ourselves questioning why we are where we are?

God can use setbacks

That call test was just one of many times I've had to fail fast, adjust my heart posture, and give it another go. God can use the hard moments to teach us and refine us into who He created us to be. He knows exactly what we need, and He has a plan when life looks much different from the life we pictured.

If it were up to us, it would be easy to count our tough seasons as a lost cause, but God can use what we see as a setback to set us up for what He is calling us to next. The same God who has carried us our entire lives is with us each and every day—even when we feel alone.

> God can use the hard moments to teach us and refine us into who He created us to be. He knows exactly what we need, and He has a plan when life looks much different from the life we pictured.

Jesus tells us in John 16:33, "I have said these things to you, that in me you may have peace. In the world you will have tribulation. But take heart; I have overcome the world" (ESV).

We may not be crystal clear on why we are where we are, but we know that we have an assignment from God right now. Let's process this truth.

I encourage you to listen to "Fires" by Jordan St. Cyr while we spend time reflecting.

1. What questions are on your mind today?

2. Describe where you are sitting in life right now.

3. How is your heart in this moment?

4. How do you want to finish your current life assignment?

5. Write down what you see as a setback in your life right now, and use this space to bring that concern to God in prayer.

key takeaways from someone who had every reason to question his position

In the Bible, David would have had every reason in the world to question why he was where he was. For this section, we're going to reference his story, which begins in 1 Samuel 16.

To set the stage: A prophet named Samuel was tasked by God to find a new king of Israel to replace King Saul. God told Samuel to go to Jesse in Bethlehem because one of his sons would become the next anointed king.

Here's how it went down.

Samuel invited Jesse and his sons to a sacrifice, just as God had asked. As soon as Samuel saw one of Jesse's sons, he thought that this son would be the next king. We see God's response to this in 1 Samuel 16:7, "But the LORD said to Samuel, 'Do not consider his appearance or his height, for I have rejected him. The LORD does not look at the things people look at. People look at the outward appearance, but the LORD looks at the heart.'"

> ## key takeaway #1:
> While we may look at our external qualifications
> to determine if we're a good fit for what God has
> called us to, God is looking at our heart. He
> knows us and calls us to exactly what He planned,
> a plan that has been in place since before we
> were even born.

Take a look at what happened next. After Jesse presented six of his other sons to Samuel, Samuel told him that God had not chosen any of those sons to be the future king. Then Jesse admitted that he had one more son who was out tending the sheep (1 Samuel 16:10–11).

Even David's own father wasn't taking bets on him being the next anointed king. But David's time tending the sheep had purpose, and God knew exactly how and where to prepare David for his future role. As soon as Samuel saw David, God told Samuel that David was the one and to anoint him (1 Samuel 16:12).

> ## key takeaway #2:
> We don't have to do anything to be more dis-
> covered or known. God is preparing us right where
> we are and will call us to what is next in His timing.
> He knows where to find us.

Imagine turning in a résumé with "Shepherd" as your title and getting a call to be the next king of Israel! How crazy is that? David was discovered by Samuel while he was showing up exactly where he was positioned—tending the sheep.

> ### key takeaway #3:
> Each one of us is chosen and set apart by God to do exactly what He planned for us. It is important to show up wherever God has placed us in this moment.

Guess where David went after this? The obvious place would be to the throne as the king of Israel, but that wasn't what God had planned. Because God works in His own timing, David went back to be with his sheep while Saul remained the reigning king of Israel. Can you imagine being told you were chosen to lead a nation, only for God then to put you right back in the fields as a shepherd?

Many believe that David was around fifteen years old when he was chosen to be the next king, and 2 Samuel 5:4 reveals to us that he was thirty years old when he became king. For fifteen years, God was preparing David for this moment.

Those fifteen years weren't exactly a cakewalk for David. His résumé during this time would have included:

- playing music for Saul, the current king of Israel
- volunteering to battle Goliath and winning that battle with a staff, five stones, his shepherd's bag, and a sling
- running for his life because Saul was plotting to kill him
- leading people through multiple battles
- dodging his own army, who wanted to stone him

I imagine David must have felt confused at times, like we do, wondering why in the world he was in those situations and how he could find his way out. I bet he felt exhausted, frustrated, and even defeated along the way.

Just as these moments were a part of God's plan for David, where we find ourselves today is a part of our plan from God. Showing up in the *in-between* seasons matters, even when a situation doesn't yet make sense to us.

first step to adjusting our heart posture

Before we go too far too fast, let's look back on how I shifted my entire perspective that day on the Peloton, just by adjusting my posture on that bike. The thing is, it wasn't just my physical position that had changed. What had really transformed was the posture of my heart.

To be clear, let's examine the definition of *posture*. *Merriam-Webster's* describes *posture* as a "state or condition at a given time especially with respect to capability in particular circumstances."[2] In other words, our "posture" represents how we are handling our current circumstances.

What does *posture* have to do with our heart?

Baker's Evangelical Dictionary of Biblical Theology explains, "The emotional state of the heart affects the rest of a person." It goes on to say, "The heart plans, makes commitments, and decides."[3]

If that doesn't make it clear to us, perhaps Proverbs 4:23 says it best: "Above all else, guard your heart, for everything you do flows from it."

All this to say, our heart is the place where our eternal spirit resides. So if our heart isn't in the right "posture," then we aren't following God's call for our life. Like how I wasn't listening to the trainer who was telling the class to lean forward and give it our all.

Just as my position on that bike impacted my performance in class, our heart's posture will directly impact the actions we take, the decisions we make, and the words we say in our daily life.

We're starting to see the full picture, right? Just as our heart's physical health is critical to living here on earth, our heart's spiritual health (or posture) is critical to living the abundant and eternal life God created for us.

The best news in all of this is that the Holy Spirit dwells inside of our heart with our eternal spirit. He is with us, always, which means we aren't left to do this life on our own.

Check out what Romans 8:9–11 tells us:

> But if God himself has taken up residence in your life, you can hardly be thinking more of yourself than of him. Anyone, of course, who has not welcomed this invisible but clearly present God, the Spirit of Christ, won't know what we're talking about. But for you who welcome him, in whom he dwells—even though you still experience all the limitations of sin—you yourself experience life on God's terms. It stands to reason, doesn't it, that if the alive-and-present God who raised Jesus from the dead moves into your life, he'll do the same thing in you that he did in Jesus, bringing you alive to himself? When God lives and breathes in you (and he does, as surely as he did in Jesus), you are

delivered from that dead life. With his Spirit living
in you, your body will be as alive as Christ's! (MSG)

When we invite Him to take up residence inside our heart, He transforms our heart posture and shifts our entire perspective, even when our external circumstances stay the same.

Can we celebrate how special this gift is? This is just the beginning of the abundant, eternal life He has promised us.

how to pivot our posture

What if the ordinary is actually the extraordinary? Life isn't about waiting for the next big thing. It's about walking in the everyday moments with God dwelling within us.

The place we find ourselves in today doesn't surprise Him. Even when we feel "stuck," God is moving in ways we may never fully understand. He has given us purpose where our feet are planted, right here and right now.

> **L**ife isn't about waiting for the next big thing. It's about walking in the everyday moments with God dwelling within us.

Not only can God use you, He IS using you. Let's strategize how we can pivot our heart posture to fully accept this sacred truth.

- ● **Step one:** Let's give our current circumstances and questions over to God. This can play out for us in many ways throughout any given day. For example, we can:

- pray out loud on the way to work or school, and invite God into our day
- listen to worship music in the bath or shower to thank God for another day
- journal about where we saw God at work in our life today
- take time to love those around us

And the list goes on.

- **Step two:** Ask God to use this place to continue to transform our heart. This allows us to shift our focus

> ▲▲ So here's what I want you to do, God helping you: Take your everyday, ordinary life—your sleeping, eating, going-to-work, and walking-around life—and place it before God as an offering. Embracing what God does for you is the best thing you can do for him. Don't become so well-adjusted to your culture that you fit into it without even thinking. Instead, fix your attention on God. You'll be changed from the inside out. Readily recognize what he wants from you, and quickly respond to it. Unlike the culture around you, always dragging you down to its level of immaturity, God brings the best out of you, develops well-formed maturity in you. ▼▼
>
> **Romans 12:1-2 MSG**

away from the confusion and suffering and onto inviting Him to work on what He cares about most—our heart.

- **Step three:** Trust that God is doing what is best for us, and embrace the resistance we are facing in this season. Lamentations 3:22–23 tells us, "Because of the LORD's great love we are not consumed, for his compassions never fail. They are new every morning; great is your faithfulness."

- **Step four:** Strategize how we want to show up and live our life in the seat that God has placed us in today by reflecting on the following questions.
  - What do you want your heart posture to be?

  - How will this new perspective equip you to give it your all wherever you are?

- What are some ways you can live out your purpose
  in your everyday?

Isn't this exciting? We're making real progress together. Now, let's meet our first friend who has learned that PURPOSE DOESN'T PAUSE.

a purposeful chat

with Aren Moore

*"You don't have to clean yourself up or make
yourself presentable or fake the life you've
lived for God to love you! He sees you right
where you are and says 'I want you.'"*

Aren Moore

Aren has a heart of gold and an incredible story that shows God's
faithfulness in her life. Right now, Aren finds herself working in a
furniture store located in Hattiesburg, Mississippi. Is this the career
she'd planned for herself? No. Is this where she believes God has
placed her for a reason? Yes. Let's learn more as she answers the following questions.

HOPE: How does confusion make you feel when you're questioning why you are where you are today?

AREN: The best way I can answer this is by giving you something
to imagine. I found out I needed glasses when I was in tenth grade. I
had no idea there was an actual problem because for years I thought
my vision was normal. I would sit in the front of the classroom and
still need to go to the board to see the notes. In middle school, I
played soccer and I remember feeling so frustrated because I couldn't

see where the ball was or which goalie was ours. The only thing clear to me was the girl to my immediate left or right. I struggled seeing my mom or dad in the stands, which often led me to assume they weren't there. I felt the weight of disappointment and guilt when my team lost because I thought it was all my fault.

When I finally got my glasses in high school, the doctor looked at my mom and said, "I don't know how she's making good grades, let alone straight A's. She can't see."

On the ride home, the trees captured my undivided attention and I was truly in awe. I had never known how detailed they actually were because for so long I'd had blurred vision. For years, I had settled for being blind and confused.

And that's how I still feel today when confusion sets it. I feel like I still have blurred vision. It makes me frustrated and angry because I feel like I am the problem. But I've come to realize this is just another tool of the enemy. If he can confuse us to the point we stop moving, then we stop stepping into our purpose. And we stop living out our true identity in Christ.

The enemy loves that, doesn't he?

When I was young, I eventually stopped moving on the soccer field because I was unsure of who had the ball and confused about which direction we were going. Most of the time I played defense, trying to deny the opposing team the opportunity to turn and attack us if they received the ball.

Now, I was no Megan Rapinoe or Alex Morgan. I only played for a year, but that experience taught me a lot of valuable lessons in regards to life.

NOW I SEE CLEARLY! The enemy knows that if he can cause us to doubt God's plan for us, then he wins. With this clarity, I am no longer afraid to try new things or to fail at them. I step into my God-given purpose each day because I can see past the confusion that kept me stuck in place.

HOPE: Which key moments in your life have made you feel most confused?

AREN: I would say three moments really shook me to my core.

- In the sixth grade: When my parents divorced, I worked after school as a janitor to help pay our family's bills. I couldn't imagine life would ever get better than what it looked like in that moment. I felt confused and hopeless.
- In college: When I became a Christian, my friends started ignoring me. I struggled to see how I would ever make it through the pain of their rejection.
- And recently: When I felt called to apply for a job at a local furniture store. I had no experience in that area and didn't know my purpose there.

Each of these moments led me to ask, "What is going on, God? I'm trying to believe You know what is best for me, but right now, I don't understand."

I've definitely had moments when I've had to remind myself that I am in the middle of an assignment given to me by God. He has a plan, even when I can't see it. So if God continues to keep me at a furniture store, then that's where I will stay. His name will be glorified wherever I am or wherever He takes me. My life doesn't have to look the way I think it should because I trust that He knows what's best for me.

HOPE: **What a wise outlook. Any final words to the girl reading this today?**

AREN: God wants to use each of us where we are at. He has purpose for you today—not just a purpose when you are where you want to be. But right here. Right now.

Isn't Aren's story inspiring? I love how she openly shares that at times she has to remind herself that she is in the middle of an assignment that God has given her. Use this space to write a prayer to God about the assignment He has you on.

Use the following prayer prompts to get started:

- Share with God what you are experiencing in the assignment He has you on today.
- Ask Him the questions that occupy your mind right now.
- Tell Him about what is confusing you in this season.
- Extend an invitation for Him to be a part of your daily life and guide you as you walk through this assignment.

when our dreams aren't what we pictured

"Sometimes to get your life back, you have to face the death of what you thought your life would look like."[1]

Lysa TerKeurst

What if we weren't made to know or understand every single detail about what the future holds for us? What if God's vision for our lives is greater than the expectations we create for ourselves?

As soon as it felt like the cloud of confusion had left my life and a glimpse of sunshine had peeked in, I suddenly found myself right back in the middle of questioning everything around me. It was like taking one step forward only to take a giant leap back to feeling even more unsure than before. The crazy part of all of this was that I was living out what I had always dreamed of, only to discover that the reality of those dreams looked much different from how they had played out inside my head. Funny how that works, right?

And then, as life tends to do, I was dealt another BIG surprise. Will and I found out we were expecting our first baby (a baby girl!). The one thing I've probably been the most confident about wanting in my life was to be a mom, and now stepping into motherhood was the single thing I was most unsure about. I'd never felt so unprepared.

It took just six months into the pregnancy to realize that my expectations of what being a mom was supposed to look like were not matching how motherhood was actually working out for me.

Have you ever found yourself feeling more alone than ever before, even while you're living the very situation you've prayed for all along?

The good news is that our unmet expectations don't have to keep hold of us.

In this chapter, we will:

- identify our expectations and where they come from
- understand what happens when expectations are unmet
- begin to blaze a new trail forward by focusing on God's vision for us
- create a plan to manage our expectations

Together, we're going to cultivate a new way of living, one founded on His promises about our future and His vision for our lives.

the skinny on expectations

We first need to understand why we have expectations and what happens inside our brains when things don't go as we planned.

According to Brigid Lynn and David Rock with the Neuro Leadership Institute, "we crave certainty and control." To satisfy our need for certainty, we set expectations based on past experiences. In other words, we imagine our future by relying on the knowledge we've gained in the past. Whatever we expose ourselves to (directly or indirectly) will impact how we see our lives playing out.[2]

How interesting is that?

Whether we realize it or not, our future is formed by what we *imagine* life will look like. This goes for our personal and professional lives. We often feel the pressure to perform based on what we *believe* is expected of us.

Research findings explain that when our expectations are met, "the reward centers of the brain are activated."[3] All those feel-good chemicals are released and we want MORE!

But there's another side to that arrangement. When life doesn't play out as we expect, our brains sound the alarm, firing those fight-or-flight chemicals that make us feel anxious. We all know how that feels—terrible!

In *Psychology Today*, David Rock elaborated further by explaining findings from a study on expectations and their correlation to dopamine (the primary chemical in our brains that makes us feel good). The work of Professor Wolfram Schultz at Cambridge University in England supports this claim. Schultz observed dopamine levels rising when our expectations were met. And dopamine levels dropping when they weren't.[4]

Even more interesting is that when dopamine levels drop, this feels similar to pain and impacts our ability to focus. Thus ... the feeling of CONFUSION! See how we are setting ourselves up to be confused? And therefore, we're setting ourselves up to feel "stuck"?

This proves my mentor knew what he was talking about when he said, "You aren't stuck, Hope. You just think you are." It really was all happening in my own head!

This doesn't just occur when big expectations aren't met. Even the simplest disappointments can cause these dopamine fluctuations throughout our everyday lives: "Expect the lights to change and find they take a long time and your dopamine levels fall, leaving you feeling frustrated. Expect the service at the bank to be fast but find a long queue, more frustration. Not only does dopamine go down in these instances, you also get a mild threat response, reducing prefrontal functioning for deliberate tasks."[5]

It's no surprise, then, that Cleveland Clinic reported symptoms of low levels of dopamine include:

- lacking motivation
- feeling tired, hopeless, moody, and/or anxious
- having a hard time concentrating
- struggling to sleep or stay asleep[6]

identifying what we thought life would look like

Expectations aren't always a bad thing—they just set us up to feel pretty bad when we're let down. The key is learning how to manage our expectations in healthy ways. But before we can manage our expectations, we need to understand where they come from.

I'll go first and break the ice.

A big part of why I feel unequipped to step into motherhood right now is that I'll likely be a working mom. This is interesting because I see the corporate world as my mission field, and I really do love to work. But in my mind, I saw motherhood playing out differently.

Where did this belief come from? My past experiences with the mothers in my life.

My mom stayed at home with me. All the other mothers in my family stayed at home with their kids. That model of motherhood is the only model of mothering I've personally experienced. So I have no past experiences to help me form realistic expectations of what life as a working mom is supposed to look like.

You may have had the opposite experiences, and you may be crushing it as a working mom (please teach me your tricks, if this is you). But I've struggled with these unmet expectations during my pregnancy and have felt so stuck—sometimes allowing that confusion to extinguish the joy of mothering.

There's something empowering about writing out these "hurdles" that are holding us back. Go ahead and play "Another in the Fire" by Hillsong United while you answer the questions below:

1. Expectation: What was your life supposed to look like?

2. Experience: What experiences led you to develop this expectation?

3. Reality: What does your life look like instead?

4. Now that you've spent time reflecting, use this space to bring your expectations and experiences to God in prayer.

let's blaze a new trail forward!

Not long ago, I rode to a conference with Maddee Hill (a friend who will share her story with us later in the book). I was confessing my worries when she looked my way and said, "Hope, you don't have to carry it all."

What powerful truth!

Over and over again throughout the Bible, we see God showing us that we don't have to carry it all.

Let's revisit the story of David we chatted about in the previous chapter. Remember how he bravely defeated Goliath using just a staff, five stones, his shepherd's bag, and a sling? How did he whip up these tools? He had them handy because he was living out his role as a shepherd, which is exactly where God had placed him when it was time for him to go up against Goliath—the brutal foe who had caused everyone else to flee in fear.

See the big picture at work here? Just as God knew exactly how to prepare a shepherd to overcome the enemy (and eventually rise up to lead his nation), God places us with intentionality and purpose every step of the way. Even though we can't yet see the longer view, God knows what is ahead for each of us.

God used my pregnancy to teach me that my baby girl is just as much His child as I am His child. I have learned to trust that He will provide what is best for her, even if that looks a little different from what I had planned. I've had to learn to trust that He will supply what we need each and every day—just as He has always done for all His children ... including David. And including YOU.

This perspective shift allows us to lighten our load and release the weight of all we are carrying and clinging to so tightly each day. It allows us to make room in our own lives to receive and embrace what He is doing in the here and now.

Even though we can't yet see the longer view, God knows what is ahead for each of us.

Let's bring back to light the two questions from the beginning of this chapter: (1) What if we weren't made to know or understand every single detail about what the future holds for us? (2) What if

God's vision for our lives is greater than the expectations we create for ourselves?

Proverbs 16:9 gives us the answers: "In their hearts humans plan their course, but the LORD establishes their steps."

As we've witnessed in our own lives, the preparation isn't always easy, but He gives us exactly what we need to take each step that He planned. Even when we can't see it (which happens often), we can be expectant and full of hope as we set our eyes on what He says about our lives.

God's vision for us

In *Systematic Theology*, Wayne Grudem taught that God is with us at all times, constantly directing us to fulfill His purposes.[7] To dig deeper into how this plays out in our daily lives, let's examine seventeen key takeaways in the Bible that show us how God directs our actions every step of the way.

Today, God is calling us to:

- SERVE HIM WHERE WE ARE PURPOSEFULLY PLACED TODAY.
    - Do good works that He prepared for us to do (Ephesians 2:10).
    - Live out His plans that give us hope and a future (Jeremiah 29:11).
    - Know that we are chosen by Him (1 Peter 2:9).
    - Be strengthened and helped by Him without fear of where we find ourselves in life (Isaiah 41:10).

- TRUST HIM TO EQUIP US WITH ALL WE NEED TO SUCCEED.
  - Go to Him to renew our strength so that we don't grow weary (Isaiah 40:31).
  - Come to Him with our burdens and in return learn from Him and find rest (Matthew 11:28–29).
  - Allow Him to lovingly instruct us and teach us as we navigate life (Psalm 32:8).

- KNOW THAT HE IS WITH US ALWAYS.
  - Never be separated from His love (Romans 8:38–39).
  - Know that He has gone before us and will never leave us (Deuteronomy 31:8).
  - Live with the Spirit that He gave us—one of power, love, and self-discipline (2 Timothy 1:7).
  - Stay connected to Him and do life with Him (John 15:4).

- DO ALL THINGS IN LOVE.
  - Love one another (John 13:34).
  - Trust Him and be filled with peace and joy (Romans 15:13).
  - Do everything as we are doing it for Him (Colossians 3:23).
  - Make disciples and spread the Good News (Matthew 28:19–20).

- FOCUS ON ETERNAL LIFE.
  - Remember that the sufferings we experience on earth have nothing on the glory that will be revealed to us (Romans 8:18).
  - Never perish and live eternally with Him in heaven (John 10:28).

It is so easy to live this life feeling defeated, but we can feel empowered by knowing we aren't alone. Just look at what Jesus said in John 10:9–10: "I am the gate; whoever enters through me will be saved. They will come in and go out, and find pasture. The thief comes only to steal and kill and destroy; I have come that they may have life, and have it to the full."

managing our expectations

Who doesn't love a good game plan? Let's come up with a way to better manage our expectations so that we can cultivate a new path forward. Here are a few steps to help us show up even when our dreams look different from what we expected:

1. Take time to understand the expectations you have and the specific life experiences that set up those expectations in your mind.
2. Communicate and share those thoughts with a trusted friend to further process your emotions.
3. Spend time in prayer to seek direction and clarity from God.

4. Identify what you are thankful for, and list out any expectations you are going to let go of.

5. Focus on God's vision for your life. Write down a few verses and the truths you are focusing on.

6. Continue to pray daily and incorporate Him into your daily life. Trust that He's got you covered and is never leaving your side.

7. Start watching for Him in your day and notice what He is doing through and for you.

8. Repeat these steps as often as you need, and remember that you are not alone in feeling this way.

It's going to be incredible to look back on this season and see just how much God showed up. His fingerprints are ALL over our lives.

It's time to meet Shelby Sanderson, who shares how she had to pivot her career plans and make a quick move to Houston, Texas.

a purposeful chat
with Shelby Sanderson

*"There's an overpass in Houston that used to say
'Be Someone' in bright graffiti. I almost wonder if
that's engrained into humanity ... We just want to be
someone, but that is not the purpose ... What if we can
use this season to relate to other people and worship
the most significant Someone of all time?"*

Shelby Sanderson

Shelby Sanderson graduated college with a psychology degree, got rejected by six out of seven graduate programs, and hadn't heard from the seventh when she decided to move forward with plans to work at a summer camp.

In the middle of the summer, her mom called to tell her she'd been accepted into the last program she'd been waiting to hear from in Dallas. Three months into that program, she realized counseling was not what she was passionate about after all. After careful thought, she decided to pivot unexpectedly and step away from the very program she'd been working so hard to get accepted into.

Since then, she has questioned why God would have allowed her to commit wholeheartedly to a five-year agenda only to let her discover this field was not the right fit for her. Despite all the confusion, she chooses to put her trust in the Lord because He's always been faithful, even though her dreams don't look like she pictured.

HOPE: Can you describe how you have been feeling during this season of confusion?

SHELBY: For me, confusion feels like a teacher asking you a question. You should know the answer. Everyone else knows the answer. But for some reason you don't know the answer. This moment seems magnified, and you feel inferior because you feel like everyone expects you to know the answer.

You feel confused. You feel judged. You feel like a failure. You feel stuck, like you're trapped in quicksand with no way out.

As you look around at everyone else, you wonder: How do they all know the right answer? How did they figure out where they wanted to live, what they wanted to do with their lives, and who they wanted to marry? How is life so easy for them when it feels so hard for me?

HOPE: What did you decide to do once you realized counseling wasn't for you?

SHELBY: My identity was shattered, and I just wanted to run back home. But I soon realized the solid foundation that I once had there was gone. My family dynamic was broken. It didn't even feel like the home I grew up in. The one thing in my life that I was certain would be solid and unbreakable wasn't.

It became clear very quickly that I was going to have to lean on the Lord and the Lord alone. There was no other place I could run to or go to other than Him. It was so hard, but so purposeful.

I started teaching through an online program. For some reason, it felt like something I could do, even though this was nothing like what I had pictured for myself.

HOPE: **What did God teach you during this season?**

SHELBY: I had a sudden realization that there is this crossover point in our life where we can no longer rely on parents, teachers, friends, or step-by-step road maps. There comes a day when we realize that all of those can fail us or disappoint us, and we have to lean on the freedom and strength from our Father.

Sometimes life feels like we've put on a backpack and are facing an upward climb on an unfamiliar mountain. I've learned that even when our dreams don't play out like we thought, He is going to sustain us. He will supply our every need no matter where He has us going.

HOPE: **Have you found anything positive from being confused?**

SHELBY: We can't solve a problem without thinking, right? This unexpected shift forced me to learn how to send out quick résumés and job applications, find a roommate, and secure an apartment.

Even though this might be one of the hardest times in life, we can use these challenges as opportunities to grow and become who

God designed us to be. We have to make moves and transitions trusting Him.

HOPE: How do you cope with your dreams looking different than you pictured?

SHELBY: I've started texting a friend about the lies that I'm believing. I might text her something like: "I feel like my life is a complete mess." Or "I feel like I can never be loved."

She allows me to share everything on my mind, and when I'm finished, she combats these lies with scripture.

I text her around four times a week, and she has even started to send me her lies so I can help her combat them with truth. Having a friend who listens and points me to Jesus has been a game changer.

HOPE: How have you learned to let go of expectations?

SHELBY: I think carefully choosing what I watch, listen to, and am scrolling past has helped. What I'm consuming directs what my thoughts are consumed with. For example, when I'm scrolling and seeing other people at different stages of life, I'm second-guessing my stage of life.

I've also learned to spend more time with people who make me laugh. You can do this too! If you can find people who make you laugh, you aren't going to spend that time worrying about your 401(k), your next job interview, and everything else in life that feels like a big question mark. This has helped me practice living in the moment and being okay with what my life looks like today.

HOPE: **How do you focus on depending on the Lord in your daily life?**

SHELBY: In Houston, I made a daily choice to depend on Him and Him alone. This helped me develop an attitude of surrender and thankfulness. He was using this time of uncertainty to create character of trust and reliance on Him that I would have probably never learned if I hadn't moved back to Houston.

I also saw Him heal my family. We went to church together every week, and each week we as a family got closer. The Lord united us again and started to rebuild that foundation for us. It was so neat to watch what He can do with small steps.

Another prayer of mine was to find a community in Houston since I was really missing the one that I had in Dallas. It was crazy, but friends randomly reached out from Dallas when I needed it most, reminding me I wasn't forgotten. It was clear that He heard my prayers and provided for my every need. That is how much He loves us.

HOPE: **What final advice do you have for the girl reading this?**

SHELBY: When I feel confused, I ask myself: What would you tell your daughter right now? Everything that I say to myself lightens and softens when I think about what I would say to my daughter with the same problem.

The Lord has this situation under control. He has a plan. We are going to look back on this season of life and be proud of how we trusted the Lord through the mess.

What an amazing story from Shelby. I love her idea of considering the advice she might give her future daughter if she were facing the same problem in her life. Go ahead and write out what you would say to your daughter here:

when something good comes to an end

"What we really have to know when we're walking into something with God is that even though we might be able to see a little bit, his ways are higher than our ways, his thoughts are higher than our thoughts, and he is going to do exceedingly and abundantly more than we could ever dream of."[1]

Sadie Robertson Huff

When I was ten years old, our family's landline phone started ringing. I sprinted to pick it up in the living room because, around three o'clock that morning, my parents had left for the hospital. My mom was in labor.

I listened as my dad gave updates through the phone. "What we talked about happened," he said.

This could only mean one thing—my newest baby brother, Gabe, who had been diagnosed with Potter's syndrome (a rare condition in which one doesn't develop kidneys) had survived his birth.

With great relief, I handed the phone to my nana and rushed to put my three-year-old brother, Hunter, in his "I'm a big brother" shirt and both my eight-year-old sister, Hannah, and me in our "I'm a big sister" shirts. We were all so excited, and to this day, I can only imagine what was going through Nana's head as she watched this scene unfold.

As soon as we got to the hospital, we hurried to meet Dad. The hallway was quiet, the room so tucked away that it felt hidden, like a secret space.

Something was off.

Had I totally misunderstood the update my dad had given me earlier on the phone? Months leading up to this, he had told me about Gabe's diagnosis and what this could mean for our family. But the worst-case scenario we'd discussed wasn't happening. How could it?

We all piled into the stark room. I stared at the white walls and sage green chairs while Dad gave us the news no parent ever imagines they're going to have to give their kids. "Your brother didn't make it."

How could God do this? Wasn't this supposed to be a miracle moment? Wasn't He a good God? These questions lingered in my mind for years.

The rest is a blur, and even reliving this moment inside my head now is proving painful. A few tears have definitely been shed here in my writing spot at Heroes Coffee in Rogers, Arkansas, today.

I bet you too have had a moment in life when you wanted to scream, "It wasn't supposed to be this way!"

I'll never understand why bad things happen, but whatever pain and brokenness you've walked through, or may even be walking through right now, please know you are far from alone.

While I wish I could jump through these pages and hug you, I can at least offer this chapter to help us navigate these hurts together. With God guiding us, maybe we can all find hope when life leaves us with unanswered questions and confusion.

Here's what we're going to do in this chapter:

- Process when something good came to an end in our lives.
- Discover more about God's character and the path He offers us.
- Focus on the encouragement written in Hebrews for those facing hard times and losing their faith.

We'll wrap up by meeting CC Calbonero, a friend who will walk us through two times in her life when good things came to an end.

time to process

Before we dive in, spend some time identifying when something good has come to an end in your own life. Work through this exercise while listening to "Rescue" by Lauren Daigle:

1. What brings us together today?

2. What questions are you left with? What are you wrestling with?

3. How did this experience impact your life? How did this change you?

4. Where have you been able to see God in this situation? How has He carried you through this? (There is no shame if you are struggling with seeing His goodness in this. I've been here too.)

5. Write down three ways you want to invite God into the situation you are in, and use this space to bring your struggles to God in prayer.

how God made a way when there was no way

What hope can we cling to when the resistance in our lives reaches an all-time high?

Today, we're going to spend some time digging into the book of Hebrews. It was specifically written for those facing hard times and struggling to keep their faith, which is exactly how I felt following the loss of Gabe. Even as a child, I had to fight off the little voice inside my head that was telling me God wasn't real.

Have you been here? Are you here now?

According to BibleProject's overview of Hebrews, the anonymous author of the New Testament book had two goals for us as we read its pages:

1. to elevate Jesus as superior
2. to challenge the reader to remain faithful to Jesus despite persecution[2]

Why would a book that was written to encourage those in hard times first focus on Jesus being greater than everything? What if it was to remind us of God's character when we don't see a way forward? What if it was to remind us of how He made a way for us when it appeared that humankind had reached a dead end?

Being reminded of Jesus shows us a beautiful picture of hope when we don't have all the answers. Let's take a look at a few key verses that can help us grasp who Jesus is:

1. Jesus is all-powerful and greater than everything. He conquered our sins and sits on the throne next to God today.

   • "The Son is the radiance of God's glory and the exact representation of his being, sustaining all things by his powerful word. After he had provided purification for sins, he sat down at the right hand of the Majesty in heaven" (Hebrews 1:3–4).

2. Jesus is able to help us.

   • "Because he himself suffered when he was tempted, he is able to help those who are being tempted" (Hebrews 2:18).

3. Jesus walked the very earth we are walking today, and because of this, He understands where we are and what we are going through.

   • "For we do not have a high priest who is unable to empathize with our weaknesses, but we have one who has been tempted in every way, just as we are—yet he did not sin" (Hebrews 4:15).

4. Jesus cried out to God and drew near to God during His days on earth. We are not alone when what we

are walking through seems too heavy. We are invited to go to Him and cry out to Him.

- "During the days of Jesus' life on earth, he offered up prayers and petitions with fervent cries and tears to the one who could save him from death, and he was heard because of his reverent submission" (Hebrews 5:7).

5. Jesus is the way we are saved and intercedes on our behalf. He laid down His life for us so that we could live.

- "Therefore he is able to save completely those who come to God through him, because he always lives to intercede for them" (Hebrews 7:25).

6. Jesus never changes. We don't have to guess where He stands or who He is. He remains the Way and gives us hope even when our circumstances change.

- "Jesus Christ is the same yesterday and today and forever" (Hebrews 13:8).

Isn't it comforting to know that Jesus can truly empathize with us? It is so encouraging to know that God sent the One who understands us most to save us.

The author of Hebrews was on to something. To be reminded that Jesus is in our corner sets a different tone. It sets a tone that

inspires us to keep pushing forward and to cling to the victory that
He has already won for us!

we've got a friend in Jesus

Please tell me I'm not the only one who has approached someone
only to find out that it wasn't the someone I thought it was. Talk
about awkward!

Typically, we wouldn't run up to someone we don't know. It is so
special that the author of Hebrews shares more about who Jesus is so
that we can get to know Him better. The more we get to know Him,
the more we will run to Him and do life with Him in our everyday.
After all, He knows us and would LOVE for us to come to Him.

Here are a few more examples from the Bible that further prove
the point that Jesus gets us:

- When we share the loss of a close friend or family mem-
  ber with Jesus, He understands. In fact, John 11 shows
  Jesus experiencing the loss of His friend Lazarus.
- When we share how we feel betrayed by someone in our
  lives, He understands. Luke 22 tells the story of how
  Peter (one of His trusted apostles) denied Him not once
  but three times.
- When we share how we feel like life isn't fair, He understands. Matthew 27 reveals how He, who never sinned,
  gave up His life for us so that we could live forever with
  Him.
- When we feel like the journey ahead is too tough, He
  understands. We see His intense emotion as He cried

out to God and asked why God had forsaken Him just moments before He died in Matthew 27:46–50.

We have a true friend in Jesus—a friendship that never ends, a friendship that doesn't change. Jesus said in John 15:15, "I no longer call you servants, because a servant does not know his master's business. Instead, I have called you friends, for everything that I learned from my Father I have made known to you."

How incredible is it that God made a way for us through the One who not only calls us a friend, but the One who has also walked this earth and experienced the suffering we are dealing with?

encouragement and key takeaways when we're facing hard times

Months ago, when I was struggling to see the good from this season of confusion, a random thought hit me: maybe we don't have to know what the light at the end of the tunnel is when we know the One who created light.

Doing life with the One who created light is much more important than having a tiny glimpse of the light ahead, right? In 1 John 1:5, we read, "This is the message we have heard from him and declare to you: God is light; in him there is no darkness at all."

Maybe we don't have to know what the light at the end of the tunnel is when we know the One who created light.

We may not always know the next step or where our trials are leading us, but maybe that is the point. We get to walk with the One who is leading us. We don't have to carry the heavy load of knowing all that is ahead. We can embrace and live abundant lives today because our future is greater than our temporary struggles. The good that has come to an end in our lives will all work together for His good (Romans 8:28).

Here's some encouragement from Hebrews that we can carry with us as we face hard times:

1. When our circumstances rock our world, we can cling to the unshakable hope we have because God faithfully keeps His promises.

   - "Let us hold unswervingly to the hope we profess, for he who promised is faithful" (Hebrews 10:23).

2. We can't lose sight of the race we are running. We can keep going and trust that our suffering today has nothing on the glory to come. His promises stand true even when our world feels like it is upside down.

   - "You need to persevere so that when you have done the will of God, you will receive what he has promised" (Hebrews 10:36).

3. We don't have to see or know each step ahead because we know that a faithful life dedicated to Him will lead to us meeting Him face to face and living eternally with Him.

   - "Now faith is confidence in what we hope for and assurance about what we do not see" (Hebrews 11:1).

4. We are allowed to release everything that is holding us back from the life we are called to. When we focus our eyes on Jesus, He will give us the strength and perseverance to keep going.

   - "Therefore, since we are surrounded by such a great cloud of witnesses, let us throw off everything that hinders and the sin that so easily entangles. And let us run with perseverance the race marked out for us, fixing our eyes on Jesus, the pioneer and perfecter of faith. For the joy set before him he endured the cross, scorning its shame, and sat down at the right hand of the throne of God. Consider him who endured such opposition from sinners, so that you will not grow weary and lose heart" (Hebrews 12:1–3).

Let's run to Him. Let's cry out and bring Him the hard stuff that we don't have answers for. Let's focus on Jesus and the promises we know to be true as we run this race that is far from easy.

Next up, we can take what we learned in this chapter and practice living out our purpose with our friend CC. We're all in this together!

a purposeful chat
with CC Calbonero

"When you turn around and count back ... all the doors that have shut, all the rejections, all the denial letters, all the relationships that didn't work out ... all of it was somehow happening for you. It's so hard to see it in the moments when you're standing in the middle of the valley, but with God, the ending is GOOD. In fact, it's better than good."

CC Calbonero

HOPE: When have you felt confused by something good coming to an end in your life?

CC: As I look back on my life today, if I turn around and just look at all the things I walked through, there were two major life moments that were the most confusing to me. The first one was my parents' divorce, and the second was losing my dream job.

HOPE: Walk us through what it was like when your parents divorced.

CC: Growing up Filipino, you just don't hear of divorces. You grow up Catholic, born and raised in the church, and it isn't heard of for many Filipino families to get divorced. I just never imagined that my parents would separate. I always thought that they were in love and that was that.

In the eighth grade, I think I was thirteen at the time, I found out my dad was moving out. I'll never forget my younger brother, who is five years younger, asking, "Why does Dad sleep downstairs?"

I told him it was because he was protecting us from the bad guys coming in. With Filipino culture there is a lack of transparency where we shy away from telling the truth, not because we don't want to hurt anyone, but because we think that will keep them safe. I know my mom wasn't disclosing the actual truth while we were all walking through it because she was trying to protect our hearts.

That was a really big season for me because I was gearing up to go into high school. I had all of these ambitions. Who you meet me as today is very similar to the girl I was in eighth grade—I had lots of fire and wanted to put my hand in several different buckets, from basketball, softball, and leadership to everything in between. Going into high school, I had all these thoughts in my head because of the divorce my family was going through.

I thought, *CC, you have two choices right now. You can run in the direction of defying all odds and beat the statistics of a child of divorced parents, or you can fall into peer pressure and go the enemy's way.*

My faith wasn't as strong as it is today, but I've always believed in God. In that moment I chose to cling to Him, even though it was so hard.

The confusing part was looking around at my big extended family. I had more than fifty-five cousins and none had experienced divorce. I felt very alone.

HOPE: How did you cope as you walked through the divorce?

CC: I kept asking, "God, why me? God, why us?" An older cousin, who is really a mentor, encouraged me to start journaling. I remember thinking, *Okay, I can't make this make sense, but I can write about it and I can just pour out my heart.*

I began to write down how I was feeling, and it became an outlet for me to ask God the hard questions. I did that, and by the grace of God throughout my high school experience, He kept bringing me the people I needed in my life.

I couldn't tell you that I had many answers until probably college. It's important to recognize that it's okay if something doesn't make sense. There are just some things we will never know the answer to, but when we cling to God, it allows us to live in a space of peace, peace that is beyond our understanding.

HOPE: How did you land your dream job, and how did it come to an end?

CC: I'd graduated with a public-health degree, and up until twenty years old, I thought I was going to be an eye doctor.

It wasn't until my senior year of college that I was like, "No, this isn't it. I know God wants me to be a leader, but not in an optometry office."

It was too late to switch majors so I just tacked on communications. After I graduated, I was applying for leadership roles with nonprofits when a mentor told me how she would blog at night while working as a full-time bond trader by day.

She hired me on full time for about two years, and it was one of the greatest experiences. I was developing my skill set as a social media manager when I didn't even know that was what I wanted to do.

Then, a friend who was working for one of the biggest motivational speakers in America texted me and said, "I don't know what you're doing, but I just have to reach out because you have been on my heart. Would you ever consider moving to work here?"

Talk about God's timing. Little did she know, I had been pleading and asking Him to show me what was next because I had no idea. I immediately said, "Absolutely, sign me up! I'll move tomorrow."

I went through the interview process, got the job, and within two weeks I'd packed up all of my college life, hopped on a plane, shipped my car, and moved to Texas.

The role was perfect for me, and I had big plans for staying there long term.

When COVID happened in March of 2020, we were all sitting inside the office and the managers told us we were going to work from home indefinitely. They told us to pack our things and that hopefully they'd see us soon. That was the very last time I would see some of the people who had become like family to me.

March was scary. We didn't know what this was going to be. I was alone in Texas, and I wanted to go home to be with my real family in California. So that's what I did.

I remember sitting in my childhood home a couple months later while being told I was being let go. Tears and tears and tears rolled down my face. Once again, I found myself asking, "Why me? Why, God? Why would You take away such a good thing? You know my heart was here. You know this was what I wanted to do for the next ten years. I wanted this so bad."

I didn't know how to move forward. It took two months of grieving for me to get over this. It felt like heartbreak, and I was so confused about what to do next.

It was that summer when a friend and I decided to start a podcast—talk about something being birthed from something that had died. If I hadn't lost my dream job, the podcast would not have happened. I wouldn't be where I am today had that door not been shut. I am so grateful now and can see how God had planned this all along.

HOPE: What would you say to someone who is trying to cope with something good coming to an end?

CC: There is fruit on the other side of the friction. I would encourage you to press on with God, even if it feels really hard. Think about the best things you have in life. Didn't most of those happen as a result of being on the opposite side of something hard?

We have to stop and think: What are we going to do with the calling that God has on our life?

HOPE: How do you live today after going through these two difficult seasons?

CC: I have learned to be heaven focused. My favorite thing to visualize is Francis Chan holding up a rope. You may have seen this before. The rope he is holding goes from one side of the stage to the other.

Francis holds up a tiny snippet in the palm of his one hand with a red piece of tape on it. He says something along the lines of this: All of this rope, that goes from one side of the stage to the other, represents eternity. This little red sliver is your time on earth. How will you spend this little sliver on earth?

This gets me so fired up. One day we'll be face to face with Jesus and that highlight reel will play. I just keep thinking of that highlight reel. I just want to die knowing that every single day, I chose to follow God's lead, even when it was hard.

HOPE: What Bible verse did you cling to in this season?

CC: God has been showing me so much around James 1:2–3: "Consider it pure joy, my brothers and sisters, whenever you face trials of many kinds, because you know that the testing of your faith produces perseverance."

God tells us to count it all as joy, so in those hard moments I just step back and say, "Okay, Lord, I'm going to reach for the joy and find the joy, even if I can't see it right now. I know You are producing something within me that could not happen if not for this moment."

Wow! What an inspiring thought from our friend CC. Take a moment to imagine your life as a highlight reel. What moments of joy can you find along your journey?

chapter 5

when you don't feel loved or good enough

"We'll never be able to wrap our minds around His extravagant love, so He gave us mountains and oceans and told us to go swim and jump and climb and, yes, put our heads out the window a couple of times. We'll never understand how grace holds us, so He gave us the wind and said to let it brush against our faces."[1]

Bob Goff

When pain and confusion set in, we may feel like we're just characters going through the motions, living out the lives we have been given but not feeling connected or engaged in any way.

We can also begin to doubt our choices, feeling as if we're making all the wrong decisions in our lives. Insecurities begin to circle nonstop inside our heads:

> What did I do?
> What didn't I do?
> What could I have done?
> What should I have done?
> What should I let go of?
> How can I break free?

The spin never ends. It feels loud even when we are in utter silence, doesn't it?

This place of confusion feels dark and lonely. Shame and guilt thrive when we find ourselves here. Before we know it, we really start to believe that we aren't loved or aren't worthy. It's hard to feel a part of anything when we don't feel loved or worthy.

Isn't it crazy how quickly this happens? We can't even put a finger on how we came to this conclusion, but it'd be hard to convince us otherwise in these paralyzing moments.

We ruminate over these questions:

> What if they find out how I really feel?
> What if my thoughts about myself are what everyone thinks about me?
> What if I can't overcome this?
> What if this is how I'm going to feel forever?

Two big problems bubble up when we find ourselves here:

1. We start believing that we can't possibly bring what we're struggling with into the light by sharing it with someone else.
2. We have a really hard time receiving God's grace, or we feel so confused that we don't understand what grace even is. (Trust me, this was where I found myself most of my life.)

About two years ago, it was on my heart to speak. It was weird because I had never spoken at a conference, and to this day, it is the only conference I've ever spoken at. We all know that God has an unexpected way of working at times. Listen to this story.

A few weeks after the desire to speak randomly hit me, my friend Nikka reached out and asked if I would speak at a local conference she was hosting. I confidently said yes without even asking the topic. It just felt meant to be.

After I said yes, she told me I'd be speaking about God's grace. Yikes. This was the very topic that always left me feeling speechless.

The longer I prepped, the clearer it became that I had never truly allowed myself to receive God's grace. In fact, I realized that maybe I didn't even understand what grace was. The perfectionist, people pleaser in me had always tried to earn God's love by proving my worth on my own.

Grace doesn't exactly work that way, does it?

Speaking about this topic felt super awkward. How was I supposed to encourage others to find God's grace when I still hadn't learned that skill myself?

I was starting from ground zero. For real—I literally had to look up the meaning of *grace*, and to be honest, I still have to remind myself of the definition often. It is so easy for me to kick back into that comfortable "earn it and prove it" mode. Can you relate?

For all you overachievers in the house (like me), here's how we can start to understand grace. Grace is the ultimate unexpected gift that God gives us, and that was made possible through Jesus' death on the cross. It is His way of saving us when we inevitably fall short (as we will all do along the way). Grace is how He extends His gift of forgiveness and love.

Grace is God choosing us and seeing us as loved and worthy no matter what. Ephesians 2:8–9 says, "For it is by grace you have been saved, through faith—and this is not from yourselves, it is the gift of God—not by works, so that no one can boast."

I still remember driving to the conference feeling unprepared and slightly embarrassed. Impostor syndrome was setting in. However, the craziest thing happened as the conference started. Nikka randomly asked the young women in the room to stand if they had ever had a hard time accepting God's grace. Nikka had no clue that I felt like I was the only one who struggled with this.

Grace is God choosing us and seeing us as loved and worthy no matter what.

As I hesitantly stood up, I looked around at a room full of standing young women. Knowing it wasn't just a "me thing" was so transformative. Do you see what this means? We are far from alone. All those insecurities that make us feel unequipped, unqualified, unloved, and unworthy ... these are the lies of the enemy!

Our journey in this chapter is going to help us go from feeling unloved and unworthy to accepting the unwavering love God has for us. Here's our game plan for discovering His grace:

- Bring what we've been walking through into the light by sharing it in these pages.
- Understand who we're up against by breaking down the first time in the Bible that we see the enemy interacting with humans.
- Create a plan to overcome feeling unloved and not feeling worthy of God's grace.

We'll then meet Ayana Symone, who will share how she broke free from feeling unloved and unworthy. She will tell us about where she has been, what God has taught her, and how she finds purpose even during moments of struggle.

bringing it into the light

What if bringing our fears into the light is actually the very beginning of stepping into the unwavering and unchanging love that is waiting for us? Before we can truly accept God's grace, we have to identify what is holding us back.

It has become evident to me over the past year or so that the root of my struggle to accept God's grace is that I tend to believe I am loved for what I do, not for who I am. For example, one of the biggest parts of my testimony that I share today is something that I hid in shame for years. I didn't think I was worthy of the scholarship I received in college. Even worse, I feared that if my friends found out I wasn't as wealthy as they were, then they would look at me differently.

Have you ever been trapped by fears or insecurities?

Your situation may be different from mine, but most people can relate to feeling unworthy or unloved at some point in life. It's your turn now. Go ahead and put on "Reckless Love" by Cory Asbury and spend some time bringing what you're walking through into the light.

1. How often do you feel unworthy or unloved? Where do you think these feelings stem from?

2. What are you walking through right now?

3. In your own words, how would you describe God's grace?

4. Where are you on your journey with receiving God's grace?

5. If you struggle to receive God's grace, what roadblock stops you?

6. Write three ways you feel unworthy or unloved right now, and use this space to bring those issues to God in prayer.

Next up, we're going to bring into the light who we are up against. If we don't fully understand or acknowledge who we're up against, we will miss out on a huge part of our strategy.

understanding who we're up against

It often feels a little weird to think about us being up against "the enemy," but what if that is the enemy's whole plan? If we don't acknowledge who is against us, how can we prepare the way we need to in our everyday lives? We can't go on pretending or just forgetting this part.

Most of the time hearing "the enemy" can make us feel fearful and a little freaked out. We have to remember as we continue on today that **God has already won**. The outcome of this battle is known, and **we're on the winning team**.

We have nothing to fear. Jesus said in John 10:10, "The thief comes only to steal and kill and destroy. I came that they may have life and have it abundantly" (ESV). Let's take a look at how the enemy first interacted with humans.

> **A**ll those insecurities that make us feel unequipped, unqualified, unloved, and unworthy … these are the lies of the enemy!

In Genesis, we learn how God created the first humans, Adam and Eve. They lived in the Garden of Eden, where God told Adam in Genesis 2:16–17 that he could eat from any tree except the "tree of the knowledge of good and evil." In Genesis 3, sin entered the world as we see the enemy being referred to as a serpent.

Here is how it all went down in Genesis 3:1–5.

Now the serpent was more crafty than any of the wild animals the LORD God had made. He said to the woman, "Did God really say, 'You must not eat from any tree in the garden'?"

The woman said to the serpent, "We may eat fruit from the trees in the garden, but God did say, 'You must not eat fruit from the tree that is in the middle of the garden, and you must not touch it, or you will die.'"

"You will not certainly die," the serpent said to the woman. "For God knows that when you eat from it your eyes will be opened, and you will be like God, knowing good and evil."

Let's take a closer look at what this interaction teaches us about the enemy:

- The enemy is crafty or clever when he interacts with us. He knows how to subtly steer us in the wrong direction by confusing us.
- The enemy wants us to question and minimize God's authority and power. The very first thing he said to humans was "Did God really say, 'You must not eat from any tree in the garden'?"
- The enemy wants us to misunderstand God and His intentions for us. If we think God is misleading us, we just might fall into the trap that the enemy is trying to lead us into. In this example, we see the enemy trying to

convince Eve that God is keeping her from eating from the tree because God wants her to miss out on being like Him.

We obviously don't still live in the Garden of Eden today, but how often does the enemy try to pull the same manipulative strategy on us? He really hasn't changed much, has he?

The enemy's strategy is simple. He aims to:

- question us
- confuse us
- convince us that we are missing out on something

As Eve painfully learned, as soon as we give in to the enemy, shame and guilt greet us. We hide our true selves in the dark, and we start believing that, due to our choices, we are unloved and unworthy.

But God knows exactly how to counter the enemy. His grace is the gift that we can receive today. The enemy knows the power we find when we receive God's grace, so he'll do everything to prevent that from happening. With faith, we can break free of the secrets and shame to truly experience God's love, knowing our worth comes from Him.

the power of God's truth

Did you know that we have access to everything we need to overcome the enemy? In Matthew 4, we learn about the time the enemy tested Jesus in the wilderness. The enemy tried to make Jesus prove that He was the Son of God. When this didn't work, the enemy tried to convince Jesus that he was missing out on a much better life—a life that only the enemy could offer him.

Guess how Jesus avoided falling into the enemy's temptation? He responded with God's Word. And guess what we still have access to today? God's Word.

Hebrews 4:12 tells us that the Bible is alive, active, and sharper than a sword. This is exactly how we're going to fight our internal battles and claim our true worth, a worth that is found only from God.

> **W**ith faith, we can break free of the secrets and shame to truly experience God's love, knowing our worth comes from Him.

I'll continue to keep it real with you—ironically, it wasn't until after the conference on grace that I started reading the Bible on my own. Up until that point, I thought the Bible was confusing and I relied on the message at church to learn more about God.

Now that we're breaking this down, does it surprise you that so many people find the Bible intimidating to read? The enemy knows that this is our weapon. It only makes sense that he wants us to leave the Bible untouched.

Our strategy here may seem simple, but it is powerful. Whenever we start questioning God's grace in our lives, we're going to combat the enemy by reading God's Word. Let's start by reading six verses about how loved and worthy we really are.

God Loves Us:

- "This is how God showed his love among us: He sent his one and only Son into the world that we might live through him" (1 John 4:9).
- "Because of the LORD's great love we are not consumed, for his compassions never fail" (Lamentations 3:22).
- "But because of his great love for us, God, who is rich in mercy, made us alive with Christ even when we were dead in transgressions—it is by grace you have been saved" (Ephesians 2:4–5).

God Chose Us:

- "Therefore, as God's chosen people, holy and dearly loved, clothe yourself with compassion, kindness, humility, gentleness and patience" (Colossians 3:12).
- "You did not choose me, but I chose you and appointed you so that you might go and bear fruit—fruit that will last—and so that whatever you ask in my name the Father will give you" (John 15:16).
- "But you are a chosen people, a royal priesthood, a holy nation, God's special possession, that you may declare the praises of him who called you out of the darkness into his wonderful light" (1 Peter 2:9).

Now, let's reclaim our true worth by learning how Ayana Symone found God's grace in her life.

a purposeful chat
with Ayana Symone

*"God knows how to take the ugly details of the past
and create redemptive new beginnings ... The creation
of the world rebels against its Creator, for example.
So the Creator comes down and dies to redeem all of
creation. That's a pretty dang good story! In that same
way, He is writing a beautiful story for you too."*

Ayana Symone

HOPE: **Tell us about a time when you felt unloved and unworthy.**

AYANA: I probably felt the most unloved and unworthy in the year 2020. It wasn't clear at the time, but I was still carrying hurt from the past that heightened how I felt during that season of my life. That made the year even more confusing.

It just didn't make sense. I'd said yes to Jesus when I was fourteen and had been owning my own faith for years at this point. But even after my decision to follow Christ wholeheartedly, I struggled with feeling unloved and unworthy off and on. I would experience these really intense anxiety attacks that wouldn't stop either.

When 2020 hit, these feelings that I'd been dealing with for years came back up and were much more intense than before. I questioned why this was happening to me. I was praying. I was going to church. I was reading the Bible. I felt like I had been abandoned, even though I knew that God doesn't leave us.

I realize now that all the confusion really came from unmet expectations. I didn't think or expect that I would struggle with fear, anxiety, and insecurities, but I was. Therefore, confusion came with my own disappointments in myself.

I knew God could heal me, fight for me, and set me free, but it felt like He wasn't doing any of those things for me. With this confusion came a lot of doubt. It just felt unfair. I was putting in the work trying to walk in faith, but it felt like He still had me there in that dark, lonely place. It was confusing to feel like I was following His path, but He still was not showing up in my life.

HOPE: What was the biggest hurdle you had to overcome? How did you overcome it?

AYANA: I would say the biggest hurdle was trusting that God was hearing my prayers. I memorized scripture that combatted my doubts, scriptures like Proverbs 3:5–6, which says: "Trust in the LORD with all your heart and lean not on your own understanding; in all your ways submit to him, and he will make your paths straight."

Living out what I knew to be true was hard during this time. I was doing all I could possibly do to try to figure out why I was struggling as much as I was.

On top of this hurdle, I started to realize that the people around me couldn't figure out why I was struggling either. When I shared with other believers that I was dealing with fear, confusion, and anxiety, they would tell me—with the best intentions and goodwill at heart—to pray more, fast more, and have more faith. The trouble was that I was already doing this. I was staying up late to pray and read the Bible, and I would still wake up with the same heaviness.

So, I just kept doing what I knew to do. I continued to pray and read my Bible. I continued to go to church. And soon, the Lord—who knew how frustrated and confused I was—finally answered my prayers. He started to reveal that I had wounds from my childhood that needed healing. These experiences from my life were the root of why I'd continued to struggle with feeling unloved and unworthy. This also helped me understand the triggers that were leading to my anxiety attacks.

When no one else could tell me what was going on, God was hearing me! And I had hope in knowing that prayer really does work, that prayer truly is powerful! I don't know why He didn't reveal my hurdles sooner, but I'm thankful that He answered my prayers when He did. Not to mention the way He showed me just how much He loves me and cares for me.

When I find myself struggling today, I continue to lean on prayer because I know I can trust Him to hear me and answer my prayers from this season of life too.

HOPE: What key takeaways from this part of your story do you carry with you today?

AYANA: I would say my key takeaway was watching Romans 8:28 play out in my life: "And we know that in all things God works for the good of those who love him, who have been called according to his purpose." He really does use all things for His good and His glory. I trust that what may seem purposeless to me is purposeful to Him.

He didn't let me walk through feeling unloved and unworthy for no reason. Today, I'm able to help others who are struggling with feeling less than or are stifled by fear because I've been there. It just goes to show that with God, even our brokenness has a purpose.

This reminds me of Psalm 139:16, which says, "Your eyes saw my unformed body; all the days ordained for me were written in your book before one of them came to be."

The second key takeaway that this season taught me is that He does listen. Psalm 138:3 says, "When I called, you answered me; you greatly emboldened me."

It may not be in the response time we are looking for, but it will come in His perfect timing.

HOPE: What are some practical tips that help you and that you think may help others?

AYANA: There are two things I do in my daily life that I think would really help anyone who finds themselves in a similar place today.

Tip #1: Ask God to reveal where the root of feeling unloved and unworthy comes from, and ask Him to heal that area of your life daily.

During my daily devotional time, I ask God to show me something in my childhood where more healing needs to be done. This has allowed me to go back to that first moment when I felt unloved and unworthy and start there. As you begin this journey, God will shower grace on you. You don't have to go through this healing journey alone.

Tip #2: Include scripture memorization in your journey to understand and remind yourself of what God has already said about you. For example, I love the truth found in Jeremiah 1:5—"Before I formed you in the womb I knew you, before you were born I set you apart; I appointed you as a prophet to the nations."

This reveals to us that God saw something in us before we were even born. He had a purpose for us and a call on our lives before we even knew what a purpose or a call was.

HOPE: What would you say to the girl reading this today?

AYANA: Do not give up. I know the feeling of thinking that this moment is the end-all, be-all. If you have breath in your lungs, it is not over. Keep going. Scripture tells us over and over to fight through the resistance and to have faith that there is something greater to come.

I may not know your exact situation, but I do know God is with you and that He can use this season to produce perseverance. You will come out stronger on the other side.

Isn't God good? As Ayana learned, He really is working actively for you and wants to see you thrive. He wants to see you walk in your purpose. He wants you to experience His love and His grace all the days of your life.

Write out the ways you see God actively working in your life today.

chapter 6 **when you feel the pressure to figure out who you are**

"It is the identity that we ascribe to God out of doubt or faith in His Scriptures that will determine the identity we give ourselves and ultimately the life that we inevitably live."[1]

Jackie Hill Perry

Do you ever feel like you just don't even know who you are anymore? Does the pressure to know who you want to be, what you want to become, and how you want to be known leave you feeling stuck and confused? No one prepared us for this part of adulthood, did they?

If you think about it, up until high school graduation, quite a bit of life was already planned for us. We knew which school grade we'd enter next, which classes we could take, which extracurricular activities we could be a part of, and who our friends would more than likely be. Our road map was pretty much set in stone, and our identity didn't change a whole lot, right?

Then after high school, we had to choose if we'd be going to college, what city we'd be living in, what career we'd be pursuing, and the list goes on. No wonder we hit adulthood and suddenly felt overwhelmed by all the decisions we had to make. Anyone else remember the top question we got asked our senior year of high school: "What are you going to do next?" Coming from the girl who didn't pick her college major until her junior year of college, this question stifled me.

The pressure to discover and understand who we are doesn't end after we graduate high school. It hits us when we take a new job, start a new relationship, meet new people, move to a new city, get married, and become a parent—just to name a few.

What if we're invited to embrace an identity that doesn't change but stays with us regardless of our season of life and current circumstances? Spoiler alert: We are more than what we've accomplished, who we know, and what roles we manage in our day-to-day.

In these pages, we are going to meet each other where we are and embrace our true identity. In this chapter, we'll learn to:

- reflect on what we've been told to believe about our identity
- discover our God-given identity—the one that never changes
- create practical ways to implement who we truly are in our everyday lives

We'll wrap up with Emma Mae McDaniel, who has learned to walk through new roles and wants to encourage you as you navigate similar challenges today.

unpacking our identity

Before we can adjust how we see ourselves, we first need to process the different identities we've been given and carry with us today. We'll take turns sharing our stories with each other here. Deal?

Have you ever been given an identity that you tried to live up to? Growing up, I was known as the "principal's daughter." You can probably imagine how teachers and peers at school treated me.

Some held me to high standards, others didn't include me, and most thought everything I received was only because of my dad's role. Isn't it sad how some people choose to focus on just one part of what makes you who you are?

I'm sure you can guess how this impacted me. I felt like there was no room to mess up, and I ultimately tried to be perfect. It's funny now, but the only nights I was popular were when the weather channel forecasted snow the next day and my peers wanted to know the likelihood of the school closing. My phone would ring off the hook!

Go ahead and share identities that were given to you and how they impacted you:

Has someone ever misunderstood your identity? The summer going into my senior year of college, my dad connected me with his friend who owned a marketing agency. The owner hired me and asked me to communicate with the CEO prior to my start date. Sounds normal, right?

Unfortunately, the CEO didn't respond to any of my emails, so I decided to show up early in the morning on my start date with a laptop in hand and ready to go. The receptionist's greeting made it obvious that she had no clue they were getting an intern. She bolted for the CEO's office to inform him of my unexpected arrival, and he didn't even come out of his office to greet me. It was a major yikes moment.

For more than an hour I sat in the lobby just waiting for someone to take me under their wing. Finally, a woman greeted me, revealed she also had no idea an intern was joining for the summer, and tried to make the most of our day by letting me shadow her. At the very end of the day, the receptionist informed me that the CEO would like me to meet him in his office.

Our introduction was short, and he was quick to ask me if I wanted to know what he thought of me.

"Sure," I responded.

"You're just some little rich girl whose daddy got her this internship," he said.

It took everything in me to hold back the tears. Little did he know, his assumption about me was far from the truth.

I wanted to tell him about my college scholarships and the three different jobs I worked during the school year to support myself and graduate with as little student debt as possible. It took me right back to high school, when I'd felt so misunderstood by others.

> **W**e are more than what we've accomplished, who we know, and what roles we manage in our day-to-day.

Unfortunately, this story doesn't end with us having a heart-to-heart and him changing his first impression. I spent the next eight weeks sitting at a small student desk crammed in a corner.

Regardless of your story, being misunderstood hurts, doesn't it?

What are some labels that others have given you that weren't true? How did this make you feel? What did you do?

We can't control how others choose to see us, but we can control how we see ourselves. Whether we realize it or not, how we see ourselves impacts how we choose to show up in our everyday.

How would you describe your identity? How does this impact how you show up in your everyday life?

who you really are

Discontentment hit me hard this year. Suddenly, the rat race didn't sound appealing anymore. Trying to climb the corporate ladder no longer sounded fun. In fact, it sounded draining.

You know you're in a bad spot when, in your twenties, retirement is already on your mind more often than not. This prompted a much-needed identity shift, one that wasn't reliant on performance, accolades, winning others over, or personal "brand."

Does this sound like a relief to anyone else?

In the midst of this identity crisis, a ministry opportunity presented itself to me. It really felt like an answered prayer and a path forward … until the logistics just weren't panning out. This was probably the hardest "no" I've ever had to give.

This experience prompted a few tough questions that we can think about together:

1. What if the place we are trying to run from is the very place that God has called us to?

2. What if we're invited to show up differently even when our circumstances remain the same?

3. What if we embraced and applied the identity that comes from Him in our everyday lives?

Listen to "Who You Say I Am" by Hillsong Worship and let's allow our true identity to sink in for a bit:

1. We are God's children, created in His image.

   - We are God's children (Ephesians 5:1–2).
   - We were created by God in His image. We were literally made to reflect and look like Him (Genesis 1:27).
   - We are fearfully and wonderfully made (Psalm 139:14).

2. We are chosen by God, who has equipped us to do His work.

   - We are chosen by God (1 Peter 2:9).
   - We are called to be the light of the world (Matthew 5:14).
   - We were created to do good works that God prepared for us (Ephesians 2:10).
   - We were given a spirit of power, love, and self-discipline—not fear (2 Timothy 1:7).

- We have freedom and are called to serve and love
  those around us (Galatians 5:13).

3. We are never alone or forsaken when the Spirit of Christ
   dwells within us.

- We are a new creation when we accept Jesus as
  our Savior. We are no longer anchored to who we
  were, what we were known for, or what we did.
  The pressure is off (2 Corinthians 5:17).
- We are ambassadors of Jesus and represent Him in
  our daily lives (2 Corinthians 5:20).
- We are friends of Jesus (John 15:15).

Write four truths about your identity that you want to cling to,
and use this space to share those with God in prayer.

This is our truth. This is who we are regardless of our relationship
status, what job we have, where we live, what family we come from,
what others think of us, and even what we think of ourselves. God
doesn't look at us and question who we are. He looks at us and sees
His children who He created to reflect His image. That is powerful,
isn't it?

living out our true identity

There is a difference in knowing who God says we are and actually applying that to our daily lives. In the book *Atomic Habits*, James Clear talked about how our habits shape our identity. He wrote, "Your behaviors are usually a reflection of your identity. What you do is an indication of the type of person you believe you are—either consciously or nonconsciously."

He continued later, "After all, when your behavior and your identity are fully aligned, you are no longer pursuing behavior change. You are simply acting like the type of person you already believe yourself to be."[2]

How spot on is this?

What we believe about ourselves guides our daily actions, habits, and how we do or don't show up where we are placed. So how do we apply our true identity to the roles and the everyday life we've been given?

Here are four practical steps we can take together to embrace our true identity:

1. Take inventory of the roles God has placed you in and the people He has surrounded you with. This includes every-thing from friends to colleagues to coworkers.

2. Write down what it would look like to live out the true iden-tity that God gives you. How would you treat others? How

would you carry yourself? What habits would you have? What actions would you take?

3. Brainstorm ways you can show up as a child of God who is called to be a light, bring love to those around you, and share the Good News in your daily life. Maybe this looks like intentionally checking on your coworkers to see how they are really doing, complimenting a stranger, or sending an encouraging text to a friend.

4. Purposefully start each day asking God to guide you to where He is calling you to shine your light and show His love.

Little did I realize that my discontentment stemmed from the identity I was trying to obtain and the self-created pressure I was carrying into my corporate role day to day. Taking the steps that we just walked through revealed that there was an entire mission in front of me that I just hadn't been able to see.

I think you'll discover the same to be true where you are today. There is breath in your lungs, people to love, and work to be done.

What we believe about ourselves guides our daily actions, habits, and how we do or don't show up where we are placed.

Maybe the discontentment or confusion around who we are is just the start of becoming who God made us to be. When we embrace the identity that He gives us, our lives begin to look different. Suddenly, life looks more like surrendering our everyday to Him and seeking Him as we take each step.

Showing up with our God-given identity looks like slowing down enough to see the opportunity He is giving us. It looks like saying a prayer over those He places in our everyday. It looks like a blend of spontaneity and surrender.

It looks like breaking through who we've been told we are and trusting God to use our daily lives to do what only He can do. It looks like obedience, and as our friend Emma Mae McDaniel will explain next, "Success is obedience."

a purposeful chat
with Emma Mae McDaniel

*"You are loved because He is love! You are beautiful
because He is your Maker! You are strengthened
because He is strong! You were made to be holy
because He is holy! We can confidently know who we
are when we confidently know the God who made us!"*

Emma Mae McDaniel

HOPE: Tell us about a season when your identity changed or
you felt the pressure to figure out who you were.

EMMA MAE: The last four and a half years of my life have been
full of transitions. I went into college single, was best friends with my
roommate, and focused on ministry. I also was writing my first books
and traveling to speak, all while taking my Gen Ed courses. And I
was sixteen hours away from home. As you can imagine, all of this
was a huge transition in itself.

It was during my freshman year that I started dating Josh. Then
COVID hit my sophomore year, so I went back home, settled into a
new routine, and published two books. Also, Josh proposed.

As I entered my junior year of college, I was planning a wedding,
continuing ministry, and living with my best friends again. But this

time, most courses had become virtual, so college continued to look different each year.

The summer before my senior year, Josh and I married and moved into an apartment together. I spent that entire summer writing because my August deadline fell right before classes started my senior year.

In this first year of marriage and my last year of college, I was trying to process the reality that school was about to come to an end. I was also trying to cherish my time with friends, knowing that we were all about to live in so many different states.

Before I knew it, graduation came. In a snap, my post-grad life kicked off with a big move back to Arkansas. And then my book came out in June.

Josh and I soon realized that making new friends and getting planted in a church wouldn't happen overnight. Now we're trying to build a new sense of normal and embrace this transition. It's a process that requires patience and trust in the Lord.

HOPE: What did God teach you during this season?

EMMA MAE: During this time, I was going to counseling. Something that I was learning was how to let myself feel emotions. This made me realize that difficult emotions aren't bad. We don't have to suppress our emotions or be perfect.

Sometimes when we are navigating transitions and stepping into a new normal, we can be oblivious to the magnitude of what we're going through. I realize now that I was expecting myself to handle all those big changes in my life like a pro. I tried to manage the transitions perfectly. In the midst of this season, God really revealed His grace to me.

I felt like He was telling me: "Emma, I am with you. All of this is purposeful. Every day of your life was written in My book before a single one of them came to be. I have not left you to hang out to dry or to figure it out on your own. In that, I need you, Emma, to trust Me."

I'm not saying we should let our feelings determine everything we do, but I am saying that whenever we're feeling overwhelmed or frustrated or excited, we shouldn't push those feelings down. If we go to God with our emotions, He can help us discover what He is trying to show us and how He is wanting to grow us.

HOPE: How did you change during this season?

EMMA MAE: When Josh and I were just a few months into marriage, I was in tears telling him that I wanted be a good wife.

He looked at me and said, "No, Emma, you're expecting yourself to be a perfect wife."

This really opened my eyes. It became clear that the pressure of what I thought others were thinking wasn't even true. Something changed when I started to voice what I thought others were expecting. Time and time again they would respond by saying, "What are you talking about? You've been doing a great job."

Through this, the Lord revealed to me that He is the perfect One. When I trust that His grace is sufficient for me, I can let go of the pressure to do life perfectly.

HOPE: What advice were you given that has helped you break free from the pressure during this season of your life?

EMMA MAE: I think back to a quote that my mom told me during college. She said, "Emma, I want to encourage you to not compare your seasons."

This really stuck with me. One example of this is making friends today versus making friends in college. In college, I met my friends literally the night before classes started. It was almost immediate. It has been a slower process to make friends in this new season.

If we compare, we can miss out on the good things that the Lord is wanting to show us now. Just because our current situation doesn't look like where we've been, it doesn't mean that it isn't as good.

I learned to embrace the change and to be willing to adapt. Over and over again, I've prayed this prayer to God: "I'm afraid of the unknown, but I trust You. I ask You to make my fears grow dim. It doesn't change the reality of my circumstances, but it does change how I am going to walk through it because I'm choosing to trust You."

HOPE: How were you able to break free from the pressure that came as your identity changed each year?

EMMA MAE: My mom told me how important it is that we don't operate from a place of thinking about what's next. This has really helped me embrace where I am in the moment.

It's so easy for us to say, "When I get to this position, then I will feel like I have arrived. Once I'm there, I will find contentment."

The secret to contentment is that we can do all things through God who gives us strength. It is in the presence of the Lord that we find the fullness of joy. When we fix our thoughts on God, we have perfect peace.

I look back and I tell you this from a place of confidence: I was just as content in singleness as I am now being a wife. I was just as content not having a single book published as I am having three books out today. I was just as content not having a college degree as I am having a college degree today.

Our identity isn't found in our titles, relationship status, or accomplishments. Our identity is found in Christ alone. While the things that we identify with may change, our identity in Him never changes.

HOPE: **What practical steps do you take to find comfort and confidence throughout the changes that come with life?**

EMMA MAE: I don't think it is a coincidence that throughout the Old Testament we see God telling His people to remember. He tells them to *remember* what He did, what He told them, and where they came from.

There was this quote that Pastor Adam Donyes once said: "Amnesia leads to doubt, but remembrance leads to a deepening of faith."

When we forget how good God is, what He says, who He is, and how He so faithfully led us in the past, we will more than likely step into a new space with doubt. When we forget all of these things, we tend to try to rely on ourselves to be perfect. We allow the fear of the unknown, fear of messing up, and fear of what people think stop us from moving forward as God intends us to do. It almost paralyzes us, if we let it.

Whenever we have a heart posture of remembrance, we can move forward knowing God never leaves us, never forsakes us, and never changes.

As Emma Mae explained, we're able to step into each new season with faith because we know who we're stepping into it with. The same is true for you!

What practical steps can you take with faith to enter into changes in your life? Are there any Bible verses or Bible stories you will remember to help you find comfort and confidence through seasons of change?

chapter 7 when you catch yourself struggling with comparison

"Nothing will kill what you've been called to do more than comparing yourself to someone else."[1]

Beth Moore

Do you ever feel like everyone around you is married, or starting a family, or traveling the world, or thriving in the place they call home, or crushing it in their job, or growing their social media following?

No one addresses the many life stages and seasons we're all walking through in our twenties. We're faced with all this pressure to have our lives figured out, but no clear map on what that even looks like.

Our road map today is going to help us break free from comparison and embrace the life God has given us. Here is what we are going to do together in this chapter:

- Understand the two different types of comparison and the impact these have on us.
- Reflect on our unique journey and struggles with comparison.
- Identify biblical truths and practice six steps that can help us break free from comparison.

We'll then meet Jordyn Price, who will walk us through her journey with comparison and share tips to help us break free in our everyday lives.

the types of comparison and their impact on us

In *Atlas of the Heart*, Brené Brown wrote, "Comparison is the crush of conformity from one side and competition from the other—it's trying to simultaneously fit in and stand out."[2]

How true is that?

We want to keep up with those around us, but at the same time, we want to leave our own unique stamp on the world. It becomes a balancing act of seeing where everyone else is, trying to identify what makes us special, and checking back in to see if we are still par for the course. Talk about stifling and exhausting!

As if learning to navigate adulthood wasn't tricky enough, there are two comparison traps that we can fall into: upward social comparison and downward social comparison.

> **Upward social comparison** is quick to point out what is missing from our lives and leaves us feeling "less than."

Downward social comparison wants us to believe we are ahead of the game when looking at someone who is a few steps behind us.

Pastor Craig Groeschel summarized the two ways we compare ourselves best: "Comparison will either make you feel superior or inferior. Neither honors God!"[3]

Before we know it, we are looking to our right and our left to identify where we think we are and where we think we should be. We don't even realize that we are comparing what God intentionally created as matchless.

So, what does each type of comparison do to us? An article from PositivePsychology.com breaks them down for us.[4]

Upward social comparison leads us to feel:

- depression/shame
- envy
- resentment
- optimism
- inspiration
- admiration

Downward social comparison leads us to feel:

- pride
- schadenfreude (enjoyment from others' troubles)
- contempt/scorn

- fear/worry
- sympathy
- pity

my struggles with comparison

Ever since my sophomore year of college, it was a dream of mine to write a book. I remember mornings when I'd ride a stationary bike at the college recreation center and jot down chapter ideas in my iPhone notes. It was a fun dream, but I didn't actually believe it would ever happen.

Comparison was quick to point out that my life didn't look like an author's life. Comparison tricked me into believing that you had to be well-known, with an interesting story and the right connections, to write a book. It felt pretty clear that classifying this as a pipe dream was the right move.

After graduating college in 2017, comparison continued to make me feel "less than." All of my college friends seemed to be thriving while I was trying to figure out what newlywed life should look like. It was Will and me, standing together against the world. Or so it seemed.

Looking back now, others probably looked at my life and wished they could find their person while I looked at their lives and wished I could find my people. Isn't it funny how comparison works?

Let's fast-forward to 2018. Will and I relocated across the country to start our careers. But after a full year of living in Arkansas, we still couldn't find our people. It sounds so random, but I decided to launch a side hustle selling clay earrings online. This was my creative solution to cultivating a community.

Each week this community would designate a theme (typically a travel destination since we were all on lockdown due to the COVID pandemic). We'd also assign a color palette for that week's collection.

What happened next still seems wild.

About a year into this venture, I decided to reach out to DaySpring, the Christian publisher and gift producer. In this message, I shared that outside of a potential earring collaboration, I also had a book idea. DaySpring said they would pass along the information to the right people.

They were probably just being nice, right? Comparison had convinced me that I was just the girl behind a side hustle, a girl who had never written a book, a girl who wasn't well-known and who still didn't have connections or an interesting story.

Writing a book was just a pipe dream, remember? At least I could look back and say I gave it a shot.

A few months went by when I randomly got a message from DaySpring's publishing team. They wanted to hear about my book idea! How crazy is that?

The rest is history. This conversation made my first book a reality and ultimately led our lives to intertwine in these pages today.

God is not limited by comparison

In the moments where we don't see Him working, God is paving a path for us. When we feel like we are falling behind, He is leading us to the very place He's designed specifically for us.

I am sure there wasn't a single person who looked at my life and thought, *Wow. Hope creating a community-centric clay-earring side hustle is really going to set her up to write her first book.* This story is a testimony to how God is always at work—not just in my life, but in your life too.

Only God can take post-grad loneliness, a side hustle, and a girl with a life that *still* doesn't look like the lives of other authors and create a path to write books.

God is not limited by the gaps that comparison points out. He isn't stifled by how we thought life would look versus how it is playing out for us in reality. He doesn't look to see where we are in relation to His other children. Instead, He looks at us and sees us exactly where He intentionally placed us. He reminds us that we were chosen for a moment just like this.

your journey with comparison

As you meet with God where you are today, play the song "Way Maker" by Leeland, and let's take some time to reflect on your journey with comparison.

1. Which type of comparison do you struggle with more: upward or downward? How does it leave you feeling?

2. In which areas of your life do you tend to compare yourself to others? Where do you feel like you are falling behind? Where do you feel like you are ahead of the game?

3. How often do you catch yourself struggling with comparison? Is there anything that helps you to break free from this pattern?

4. What does comparison point out to you? How does this impact how you show up and live out your daily life?

5. Write three ways you compare yourself to others today, and use this space to hand those over to God in prayer.

Just to keep things real with each other, comparison continues to be an ongoing struggle for me. I've caught myself comparing myself to others in terms of my pregnancy, my career trajectory, my social media following, and my relationships. And if I'm really honest, I still feel a bit like an impostor having a full-time corporate job and publishing books. I mean, who am I to think I have what it takes to manage a team? To write a book? To mother a child? These doubts and insecurities can get the best of me when I forget that God has placed me in each of these roles for a reason. But I find peace in trusting His plans for me and knowing His PURPOSE DOESN'T PAUSE.

the truth and our choice

What if we don't have to look at those around us to see if we're on track? What if we don't have to wait to live our life until we have it all figured out? What if we can surrender where we thought we would be and embrace the life God is giving us today?

> **G**od doesn't look to see where we are in relation to His other children. Instead, He sees us exactly where He intentionally placed us. He reminds us that we were chosen for a moment just like this.

Let's shine God's light on some of the common areas where we catch ourselves struggling with comparison. Focusing on His truth will help us take another step toward breaking free from comparison. Go ahead: Put a star by the verse that you're going to carry with you today.

When you start to wish you had someone else's gifts and talents, remember this verse:
"There are different kinds of gifts, but the same Spirit distributes them. There are different kinds of service, but the same Lord. There are different kinds of working, but in all of them and in everyone it is the same God at work" (1 Corinthians 12:4–6).

When you feel like giving up because it looks like you are falling behind, remember this verse:

"Let us not become weary in doing good, for at the proper time we will reap a harvest if we do not give up" (Galatians 6:9).

When you question where you are and how you're going to get to where you thought you would be, remember this verse:

"Trust in the LORD with all your heart and lean not on your own understanding; in all your ways submit to him, and he will make your paths straight" (Proverbs 3:5–6).

When you think your life looks like a mess and nothing is going right, remember this verse:

"And we know that in all things God works for the good of those who love him, who have been called according to his purpose" (Romans 8:28).

When you feel like your life is purposeless and random, remember this verse:

"'For I know the plans I have for you,' declares the LORD, 'plans to prosper you and not to harm you, plans to give you hope and a future. Then you will call on me and come and pray to me, and I will listen to you. You will seek me and find me when you seek me with all your heart'" (Jeremiah 29:11–13).

When you think your life is moving slow and you've been forgotten, remember this verse:
"The Lord is not slow in keeping his promise, as some understand slowness. Instead he is patient with you, not wanting anyone to perish, but everyone to come to repentance" (2 Peter 3:9).

Are you starting to see that we have a choice? We really can break free from the hold that comparison has on us.

Here are six practical steps that each of us can apply in our everyday lives:

1. Identify areas of your life in which you compare yourself to others.
2. Write down who you are comparing yourself to, what you are noticing, and how this makes you feel.
3. Find a Bible verse that shines God's light on what you are struggling with. Focus on the message as you write it out and memorize it.
4. Let go of comparison by cheering on the person you are comparing yourself to. This may look like sending a quick text to a friend, commenting on someone's social media post, or even sending a letter—whatever feels right to you.
5. Spend time prayer journaling about where you are and what you are struggling with. Invite God into your day.

6. Wrap up by writing down things in your life that you are thankful for today and a quick sentence on what showing up is going to look like for you this season.

Look at how far we've come. You are crushing it! Now let's meet Jordyn Price, who will tell us how comparison played out in her life, and how she learned to overcome it.

a purposeful chat
with Jordyn Price

*"Don't fall for the lies that comparison tells you!
Most people only post or talk about their best days.
The reality is, everyone has hard seasons and good
seasons. Try to enjoy and grow in your season, and
stop focusing on what others are doing. Ask yourself:
How can I show others the love of Christ? How can I
honor God today? When I turn my focus from 'look
what I don't have' to 'look what all God has blessed
me with,' it helps me be more grateful."*

Jordyn Price

HOPE: How would you describe your struggle with comparison?

JORDYN: I became a mom this past summer, and it has been the most joyous yet challenging time of my life. I love my daughter and want to be the best version of myself for her.

But as I spend time on social media, I can't help but get sucked into comparison. I notice how quickly other moms "bounce back" to their pre-pregnancy bodies, and I start questioning why I'm not there yet. I see other moms who seem to be so put together. These moms appear to do all of the cooking, cleaning, and errands, all while looking beautiful and effortless. Most days I'm still in my pajamas in the afternoon.

Other moms seem to know all the answers when it comes to their children, and I have to Google multiple things a day. The list can go on and on. It all leads back to comparing myself and feeling less than as a mother and a woman. It leaves me feeling empty.

HOPE: How does comparison hold you back?

JORDYN: Comparison takes away the joy from this beautiful season I'm in. Rather than focusing on growing, comparison makes me believe I'm not enough and that someone else is doing it better. Comparison makes me feel defeated. It's self-sabotaging. When we really think about it, comparison is a false story we tell ourselves.

HOPE: How have you broken free from comparison?

JORDYN: I remind myself that I'm exactly where I am supposed to be, just as God has you exactly where you are supposed to be. It also helps to acknowledge that social media is never the full picture. When I'm scrolling, I can choose to be happy for other people's accomplishments and to be okay when my life looks different from someone else's.

When I feel comparison creeping in, I remind myself of all the blessings in my life today. This really helps. For example, my body may not be back to my pre-pregnancy body, but instead of feeling defeated, I remind myself that my body grew and nourished my daughter. My body is able to sustain her and play with her daily. That's no small thing!

HOPE: Are there any Bible verses you focus on when comparison sneaks into your life?

JORDYN: My favorite verse is "Do not conform to the pattern of this world, but be transformed by the renewing of your mind. Then you will be able to test and approve what God's will is—his good, pleasing and perfect will" (Romans 12:2).

This verse reminds me not to get my encouragement from other people because that will never fulfill us. Only Christ can fill the emptiness that we experience. When we stop comparing, we can experience true joy and growth in our lives. We can then help others grow in their lives too.

What a meaningful message Jordyn has given us. She reminds us that our healing isn't all about us. It's bigger than us. It's about the people we'll be able to help after we learn to break free of the enemy's lies. Isn't that amazing?

What lies from the enemy are you working to break free from? What actions do you plan to take to help you find freedom from comparison?

chapter 8
when your life feels out of control

> "A sincere faith in Jesus and all
> He wants to do around us wakes
> us up, rattles our lives, shifts
> every perspective, issues hope
> in pain, and ignites purpose."[1]
>
> **Jennie Allen**

Do you ever feel like your life is going at a speed you can't keep up with? Do you ever wish you could press a pause button to catch a quick breather and get a grip on things?

We all know how it feels when life spins out of control. One thing after another happens, and before we know it, we don't even know what to do. It's paralyzing. The control we thought we had is stripped away from us, leaving us feeling forgotten, frustrated, weary, and hopeless.

Just this past week, not one, not two, but three people have listened to me share about the situations going on in my life right now and lovingly responded with "Hope, focus on what you can control."

The first time, this advice was easy to ignore. But the second and third times, it caught my attention. These people didn't know one another, so there was no way they could have tag-teamed about this message. Clearly, God wanted me to listen.

You're not going to believe this … but while writing this book, I found myself caught in another work situation that was quite different from the one we chatted about in the first chapter. Since that time, I'd taken another new role within the same company. What seemed promising, though, soon felt like a dead end.

Essentially, a senior leader was not very encouraging or accommodating when members of the team were starting their families. This was especially concerning because I'd accepted the role just a few weeks before finding out I was pregnant. To add to the frustration, my employer announced maternity leave would be changing from sixteen weeks to twenty-two weeks for all babies born, adopted, or fostered from February 1 onward. While this was a HUGE move forward for the company, guess when Baby Harris's due date was? January 27!

I was suddenly overcome with fear that I would miss out on six extra weeks with my sweet girl by a mere three business days.

You should have seen my doctor's face when I asked if there was any way we could try to make Baby H bake for a few extra days. She laughed and said, "Hope, this girl will come whenever she wants. We have no control."

There was that word again. *Control.*

What if this whole time I'd been grasping for something that was unattainable? What if the lesson was about releasing my need for control?

The best way to describe feeling out of control takes me back to studying abroad in Switzerland. One weekend our group went to a tiny ski town in the Swiss Alps. I had skied once in Utah, so surely I was ready to take on the Alps, right? It's okay to laugh. I'm laughing too. Rookie mistake, right?

As our group put on our gear and took the lift to the mountain, it became clear the conditions weren't for beginners. We were facing whiteout conditions and couldn't see where we were on the slopes. It was like fog, but worse, and totally took away my depth perception. I had no idea how to get myself safely down that mountain.

Unlike my experience skiing in the States, the path down wasn't well-marked. The stakes were high, and I easily could have found myself with a serious injury. Or worse.

I knew I was in trouble when a girl who had skied her entire life wiped out, started crying, took off her skis, and decided to scoot down the mountain on her bottom.

Isn't this how life feels sometimes? As if we've somehow found ourselves in conditions that we're not prepared to handle? There are no clear directions showing us the way forward, and it feels as if one misstep could be the end of everything. The situation feels debilitating. It's taking everything in us not to just throw our hands in the air (or take our skis off) and quit.

Maybe not having the ability to control everything in our lives isn't a disadvantage, but an intentional invitation to walk a little lighter and smile a little more by surrendering our lives to the One who is in control.

This is the journey we're going to walk through together today as we learn to:

- break down where life has you today, so God can meet you where you are
- identify what we can control and how we can find freedom
- learn more about God's character and come up with practical steps to help us surrender our daily lives to Him

We'll wrap up by hearing from our friend Emma Brownawell, who will share her testimony about a time when her life felt out of control.

where you are today

It's your turn to share what you're walking through. Play the song "Highlands (Song of Ascent)" by Hillsong United and let's meet each other where we are.

1. What circumstances are making you feel like your life is out of control?

2. How is this season making you feel in your everyday life? Feel free to share your own analogy like I did with the whiteout skiing story.

3. What unknowns keep you up at night? What is out of your control?

4. How are you coping with this right now?

5. Write two things you catch yourself trying to control in your life today, and use this space to bring those to God in prayer.

what we have control over and how to pivot our focus

Control gives us a sense of safety and comfort, convincing us that everything is on track and in order. When we no longer have a sense of control, we'll do whatever it takes to try to feel like life isn't spinning around us, won't we?

You could say that, right now, there has been quite a bit of house cleaning and organizing going on in my life lately. Do I like cleaning and organizing? Not particularly, but it gives me a sense of control when everything else in life feels chaotic. I even packed Baby H's hospital bag at thirty-one weeks pregnant just to make me feel like maybe I was somehow prepared to become a mom.

What is your go-to activity when you're searching for some sense of control in your life?

Remember the advice those three people gave me? I've been thinking about that a lot lately as I try to focus on what I can control.

But what if we expand this to find a sense of real comfort when things feel out of control? Let's do this by revising the advice to say: Focus on what you can control. And practice handing the rest over to God.

The problem with our lives feeling out of control isn't revolutionary; it's simply the lack of control in our everyday lives. Handing over what we can't control and relying on God, the One who does have control, provides a solution that we cannot fabricate no matter how hard we try.

Our first step is to process what we actually can control.

What can you control in your life today?

I don't know about you, but my list feels pretty short:

- my attitude and how I show up where God has placed me
- how I treat and love the people around me
- my communication and relationship with God

This list makes me think back to our unshakable, God-given purpose that we discussed at the very beginning of our journey— love God and love people. That's right. Our purpose isn't to control every situation and freak out when things don't go as planned. It isn't to keep everything on track and carry the heavy load that comes with that. It isn't to be held back and stop showing up until we're given a clear path forward.

Hebrews 12:1–3 says:

> Therefore, since we are surrounded by such a great cloud of witnesses, let us throw off everything that hinders and the sin that so easily entangles. And let us run with perseverance the race marked out for us, fixing our eyes on Jesus, the pioneer and perfecter of faith. For the joy set before him he endured the cross, scorning its shame, and sat down at the right hand of the throne of God. Consider him who endured such opposition from sinners, so that you will not grow weary and lose heart.

Go ahead and underline, star, and circle what pops out to you in those verses.

Focus on what you can control. And practice handing the rest over to God.

Now let's visualize my avid skier friend who wiped out in the whiteout. What did she do? She accepted where she was, threw off her skis, and found another way to get down the mountain. She just might have been on to something.

Our journey isn't always going to have us looking Instagram ready, showing our good side with a smile on our face wearing our favorite athleisure gear. Sometimes we'll have to just blindly trust there is a path forward, even when we can't see it with our own eyes. Sometimes we'll have to depend on God's promise to carry us. Sometimes we're going to have to cry out and allow Him to show us the way.

He listens to us, He carries us, and He equips us. He is in control of the journey He established for us. He is all we need.

The unknown author of Hebrews is encouraging us to focus our eyes on Jesus and hand over everything that is holding us back. The story puts into perspective the life we've been called to and challenges us to deepen our faith when we're faced with resistance. We not only have something greater to look forward to; we get to rely on the One who took control of our future and made it possible to someday step into eternal life with Him.

Are you starting to see this beautiful picture with me?

Maybe life doesn't look like a step 1, step 2, and step 3 approach that feels logical to us. Maybe life looks a whole lot more like a Google Maps reroute, one in which we trust that the right steps will be given to get us where we need to go.

> **W**e not only have something greater to look forward to; we get to rely on the One who took control of our future and made it possible to someday step into eternal life with Him.

We are invited to walk with the Lord, to focus our eyes on Jesus, and to live out our true purpose: love God and love people.

It's really that simple. We don't have to make this so hard on ourselves anymore. We can throw off the heavy load that is weighing us down right now and rest in the peace that God offers us, all by trusting He is in control.

how to hand it over

Before we practice surrendering control to God, let's look at four verses that reveal God's character as He guides us through this life:

- "'For my thoughts are not your thoughts, neither are your ways my ways,' declares the LORD" (Isaiah 55:8).
- "As the mountains surround Jerusalem, so the LORD surrounds his people both now and forevermore" (Psalm 125:2).
- "The LORD himself goes before you and will be with you; he will never leave you nor forsake you. Do not be afraid; do not be discouraged" (Deuteronomy 31:8).
- "Peace I leave with you; my peace I give you. I do not give to you as the world gives. Do not let your hearts be troubled and do not be afraid" (John 14:27).

What verse stood out to you? Why?

What are some ways you plan to start handing over what you cannot control to God?

Look what we just did. We proved that our lives aren't out of control. They are actually in the hands of the One who created us and the One who has carried us the whole time.

Would you have honestly planned out the path you are on today?

- Think about all of the blessings you never imagined receiving.
- Think about all of the people God has placed in your life that you never would have imagined meeting and knowing.
- Think about the experiences that make up who you are today.

We don't have to continue feeling like we are free-falling. We are invited to walk freely with Him down the unshakable, purpose-filled path that He designed for us. Some days are going to feel like we are on the side of a slippery mountain in whiteout conditions, holding on to skis that are only making our journey harder. Some days we're going to have to slow down, hand over what we can't control to God, and analyze where our focus really is. We're not playing the short game here. We're running a race that leads to eternal life.

Here are four practical steps we can apply in our everyday lives so that our fear of losing control doesn't hold us back anymore. The good news is that we've already practiced these together today:

1. Identify what you can control and what you can't control.

2. Practice handing over what you can't control to God by filling in these blanks:

    "God, I give (insert what you can't control) over to You. I trust that You have this part of my journey covered because (insert reason from a Bible verse that reminds you of God's true character)."

3. Spend time reflecting on how God has provided for you and led you through your life. Write down the blessings He has given you in your life and how He has provided in ways you never would have dreamed for yourself.

4. Find a space and time that you can communicate with God about your daily journey in this season. This can look however you want it to—it can be prayer journaling

while listening to music, going to a coffee shop and praying silently, or even driving to work and praying out loud.

Now we get to hear from Emma Brownawell, who will share advice and encouragement to help us walk in freedom today.

a purposeful chat
with Emma Brownawell

"Embrace the millions of little miracles that happen within a twenty-four-hour time span. If we look for God in the small moments, we will live a life of abundance. There is nothing small if God is in it. He has everything under control even when our lives make us think otherwise."

Emma Brownawell

HOPE: Tell us about a time or season when your life felt out of control.

EMMA: I've felt confused and out of control many times, but the biggest time for me was right after I graduated from college. I was working for a fashion blogger and dating someone who lived in Boston. Since I was working virtually, I could choose to live anywhere I wanted.

I really thought Boston was going to be my new home. I had a friend who lived there and we agreed we'd be roommates. That was the plan, until I found out that she had signed a lease with someone else. I remember finding out and feeling so confused. I even remember praying, "God, I do not understand why this is happening. I felt like You were guiding me to Boston. I had found a roommate, a church, and all of the other logistics were figured out. Why are You closing this door?"

After this happened, I went through a breakup with the guy in Boston. Suddenly there wasn't a single thing in my life that felt set in stone anymore. I remember telling God, "Please take the reins on this one."

Two weeks later, I got an email about another job. This unexpected opportunity changed everything for me.

It was clear that this was the job I was supposed to be in. I resigned from my other role and let go of the idea of living in Boston. I packed my bags, moved to Louisiana, and am still in this job today.

HOPE: What did God teach you when it felt like everything in your life was out of control?

EMMA: Oftentimes, when we surrender the things in our life to God, that is when He works the best. We can let go of control because we can trust that His way is so much better than our way. During this time, I would often go back to Scripture and read Psalm 119:105, "Your word is a lamp for my feet, a light on my path."

I'll be the first to admit that this can sometimes feel like the flashlight version in the middle of confusion. However, when He tells us that He is the light to our feet, we have to trust that He is making a way even when we don't clearly see it. God taught me to surrender each time I had the desire to be in control of how things would work out. He taught me to trust His promises and look to Him for direction.

HOPE: What encouragement do you have for the one who is struggling to see God at work in her life today?

EMMA: Esther 4:14 is a verse that immediately comes to mind. It says, "And who knows but that you have come to your royal position for such a time as this?"

This verse is an important reminder that God has placed us with purpose right here and right now.

Did you know that God is not mentioned ONCE in the book of Esther? Although He isn't mentioned, His fingerprints are all over Esther's story.

I truly believe that one reason Esther's story is in the Bible is to support our faith journey. There will be moments in life when it doesn't seem like God is on the scene and you have to have a firm belief that He is working in the background with every piece of the puzzle.

Even when you can't feel Him, you can still learn to have faith in Him. Even when it seems like He's absent, you can rest assured that He is present.

Walk in trust knowing that you were made for a time such as this.

HOPE: Can you share some practical tips that you learned from this season?

EMMA: God put three things on my heart that I still go back to today.

#1: Choose to be planted. Make the choice to show up for your people, for your job, and for your church.

#2: Steward the season you're in—that goes from gifts and talents to friendships and relationships. When you make the choice to steward what He has given you, make the choice to steward it well.

#3: Serve the season that you are in. Serve the best you can and serve any way that God puts on your heart.

HOPE: Any final encouragement on how to embrace the moments that God gives us today?

EMMA: Life's a wild ride but a really sweet one if you let it be. You don't have to know where you'll be in five years. You have God taking care of that. All you're called to do is embrace today.

I heard this message that if we live only for the big moments, we are theoretically missing out on 98 percent of life.

I love how in Zechariah it says do not despise the day of small things. Don't look at seemingly minor accomplishments as unimportant. Don't despise apparently insignificant, humble moments. The kingdom of God starts with a small mustard seed, which then grows into a big tree. There is nothing small if God is in it.

Nothing you do for God goes unnoticed or unrewarded. So, cheers to embracing the small moments and trusting that He is in control.

Isn't that a strong message? Emma teaches us that we can all celebrate the little things along the way.

What little things in your life can you celebrate today? How can you embrace the daily moments that God gives you?

when you are in a season of waiting

> *"You see, we're all called to wait because we all live right smack dab in the middle of God's grand redemptive story … Waiting on God is an action based on confident assurance of grace to come."*[1]
>
> **Paul David Tripp**

Waiting is hard regardless of what we're waiting on, isn't it? It isn't always very easy to see how God is working, and we may even start to question if He is working in our lives at all.

Are you waiting for clear direction about what step you are supposed to take next? Maybe you're waiting for God to tell you what decision to make regarding a significant other, a new place to live, a baby, a job, or accomplishing the dream that has been placed on your heart. The list is endless.

I'm here to tell you, I've been there too.

Eight days before college started, my entire perspective changed on how God works in the waiting. It had been my dream since the sixth grade to attend Pepperdine University. My grandparents had both grown up outside of Los Angeles and filled me in on this beautiful college nestled in the Santa Monica Mountains and overlooking the Pacific Ocean in Malibu. The only piece that wasn't dreamy about it was the price.

Let's be real. Pepperdine was a far-fetched fantasy.

As college-acceptance letters rolled in and financial-aid offers were finalized, it became clear that I had only one option: Arkansas Tech University (ATU). It was official. Pepperdine really had been *just* a dream.

Attending ATU was a done deal. I soon had a roommate, class schedule, dorm room, and even a student ID card. At this point, the only waiting going on in my life was waiting to move to Russellville, Arkansas, to start my freshman year of college.

Even my mom accepted the reality of where things had landed and sent this note to Pepperdine's admissions counselor on June 3, 2013:

> *I am so thankful for Pepperdine's generosity, but the gap between what is offered and what our family can afford is still just too large. Could we go ahead and begin the process of refunding us the $750.00 pre-tuition payment we made on May 1?*

> *I cannot express my gratitude for all you've done*
> *to help our family in this process. I am sad the door to*
> *Pepperdine did not open more fully for Hope to attend;*
> *however, I trust that God has placed her where He can*
> *use her for His glory at Arkansas Tech University.*

Over a month had gone by without a response. Then over two months had gone by without a response. As you can see, Pepperdine was just a "what could have been" at this point.

You'll never believe what happened next.

It was August 6, 2013. Just an ordinary summer day. Or so it seemed. I'll never forget sitting on the couch, watching the two little girls I babysat each summer, when my mom called my iPhone. This was the call that would change it all.

Before I could even finish saying the word hello, my mom said, "Hope, you're never going to believe this. Pepperdine just told me that you have received an additional scholarship from anonymous donors that will allow you to attend. If you want to go, we have to call and get you a dorm room today. We have eight days until we need to be in Malibu for you to start new-student orientation. Can you believe this?"

To this day, I don't remember how the conversation went after this. How was this possible? The whole time I was waiting for college to start at Arkansas Tech University, God had been making a way for me to attend Pepperdine.

Even though our seasons of waiting may look very different, this I know to be true: Before we were born, God intricately and intentionally prepared a plan that was full of purpose for our lives. This plan isn't suddenly on hold or thrown out the door when we enter a season of waiting.

When we feel frustrated, stuck, disappointed, forgotten, and anxious, God is working in ways we can't always see, feel, or understand. He opens doors that only He can open in His perfect timing. His ways don't always make logical sense to us here on earth. His ways are higher and mightier than anything we could imagine.

He is a God who uses the unexpected and the unthinkable to change it all.

As we chat about this story more than ten years after it happened, it reminds me that somehow, someway, He is working in the waiting that we find ourselves in the middle of today. There is no such thing as time wasted when we're walking with Him. Even when it feels like the clock is ticking and there is no way forward, it isn't too late for Him.

In my current situation, I have to remind myself that God is not stuck, surprised, or perplexed by our seasons of waiting. He is with us and paving a way for us right here and now.

> **Before we were born, God intricately and intentionally prepared a plan that was full of purpose for our lives. This plan isn't suddenly on hold or thrown out the door when we enter a season of waiting.**

Today, we're going to break free from how we think about waiting and find freedom in how we can live out our seasons of waiting differently. In this chapter, we'll:

- unpack your season of waiting
- explore how we can pivot our perspective on waiting
- identify ways we can practice growing and seeing progress in our seasons of waiting

We'll then hear from Allyson Golden, who will share how she is walking through a season of waiting.

your season of waiting

Let's first unpack your season of waiting. Play the song "Wait on You" (feat. Dante Bowe and Chandler Moore) by Elevation City and Maverick City Music, and spend some time reflecting on where you are today.

1. Describe the season of waiting you are in today.

2. How does waiting make you feel? Do you feel like your life has purpose in this season?

3. What thoughts have occupied your mind throughout this season of waiting?

4. How would you describe the pace of your life today? Does it feel like your life is paused?

5. Do you see God at work in your life right now? Why, or why not? If you see Him at work, share how you see Him working today.

6. Reflect on a season of waiting that you've walked through. How did God show up? What did you learn during this season? How did your season of waiting end?

7. How are you living or showing up during this current season of waiting? How do you want to live or show up right now?

8. Write three things you are waiting on today, and use this space to bring those to God in prayer.

seeing waiting in a new way

What if we didn't think of "waiting" as a season of being stagnant, but started thinking about it as a season of growth? What if we actually shortchange ourselves when we try to hurry through waiting?

Interestingly enough, the *Merriam-Webster* definition of *waiting* is "to remain stationary in readiness or expectation."[2] When we read this, it becomes clear that the world defines waiting as simply sitting still, ready for our own expected or desired outcome to come to fruition.

The problem with waiting is that the world around us conditions us to hurry.

We get packages delivered at record speeds. We call restaurants ahead of time to get seated as soon as we arrive. We go through the drive-through so we can get our coffee quickly and make it to work on time. When we have to wait too long, our default is to remove ourselves from the uncomfortable situation.

Our culture teaches us that waiting isn't a good thing; it is seen as a waste of time.

But what if we looked at waiting in a different way?

I'm the first to admit that waiting isn't easy. In my season of waiting, I had started fighting the desire to shut my laptop and quit my job. If there hadn't been bills to pay, the waiting game would have been over. I would have opted out.

But when I felt like giving up, I would remember what God said to the prophet Habakkuk when he asked how long he'd have to wait for God to do something about his situation. He wanted God to bring justice to the evil that was happening around him, and he felt like he wasn't being heard.

This is how God responded in that Old Testament story: "Look at the nations and watch—and be utterly amazed. For I am going to do something in your days that you would not believe, even if you were told" (Habakkuk 1:5).

The same God who responded to Habakkuk is the same God we're invited to do life with today. God is at work right now, doing something in YOUR days that you would not believe, even if you were told.

Little did Habakkuk know that this verse wasn't just giving him a glimpse of how God was going to overcome the situation. This verse was likely foreshadowing Jesus coming to overcome every single battle that we find ourselves in today.

How incredible is that? Habakkuk was just thinking about what he was in the middle of, while God already had a winning plan for every situation and battle that we would ever encounter.

God is at work right now, doing something in YOUR days that you would not believe, even if you were told.

God continued in Habakkuk 1 to share how He planned to overcome the evil; however, His game plan didn't make sense to Habakkuk. He went back to God full of confusion, as he questioned how this could possibly be the solution that he'd been waiting on. In response, God instructed him to write down this revelation and to *wait* for it to happen.

Guess what God didn't promise? He didn't promise that the wait would be over quickly. He actually warned that it might linger. He also said that a righteous person will live by their faith (Habakkuk 2:2–4).

This message gives a new meaning to how the world defines waiting, doesn't it? Let's redefine it together.

- Waiting is embracing where God has us today and allowing the in-between moments to stretch us and shape us.
- Waiting is remembering His promises when we feel unheard, forgotten, and stuck.
- Waiting is inviting God into our daily lives and tuning in to what He is doing.

- Waiting is trusting that He is with us and will provide in His perfect timing.

I think back to my situation at work and wonder—how many times have I missed what God was actually doing around me because I was too caught up in feeling forgotten, vulnerable, or unfairly treated?

Want to know some good news? It's never too late to pivot our perspective on waiting.

When we feel like running away from our seasons of waiting, we can instead run to the One who will do something that we wouldn't believe, even if we were told. Instead of allowing the waiting to bog us down, we can look for what God is teaching us and start to see the progress of where we were and where He is taking us.

Isaiah 43:18–19 says, "Forget the former things; do not dwell on the past. See, I am doing a new thing! Now it springs up; do you not perceive it? I am making a way in the wilderness and streams in the wasteland."

applying our new perspective

When we feel like our purpose has been paused, God has a plan. Waiting is where progress is being made on our behalf by our Creator. Waiting is where He is not only making a way, but where He is preparing us for the path ahead.

> **I**t's never too late to pivot our perspective on waiting.

So, how can we break free from how we saw waiting at the beginning of our journey today? Let's practice applying some of the key takeaways from Habakkuk and God's interaction:

1. Go to God with your waiting. You're invited to fully share how you feel, even if it isn't pretty.
2. Remember what God said in Habakkuk 1:5: "Look at the nations and watch—and be utterly amazed. For I am going to do something in your days that you would not believe, even if you were told."
3. Find ways you can watch and wait on the Lord in your daily life. Write down where you see Him working and what He is teaching you through this season.
4. Just as God asked Habakkuk to write down the revelation He revealed to Him, you can recenter your attention and write down what He promises you in your waiting. Here is one example of a verse full of truth you can cling to today:

> Do you not know? Have you not heard? The LORD is the everlasting God, the Creator of the ends of the earth. He will not grow tired or weary, and his understanding no one can fathom. He gives strength to the weary and increases the power of the weak. Even youths grow tired and weary, and young men stumble and fall; but those who hope in the LORD will renew their strength. They will soar on wings like eagles; they will run and not

grow weary, they will walk and not be faint. (Isaiah
40:28–31)

5. Embrace where God has you today, and practice living
by faith. Allow Him to teach you and stretch you so you
are prepared for what's next. You can practice trusting
that He is working in ways you wouldn't believe even if
you were told.

We're going to save some space here for you to come back and
write how God works through this season of waiting. It'll be so neat
to reflect on how He used this time to prepare you and to be blown
away by what He is doing in your life right now.

Questions to come back to:

1. What did God teach you through this season of waiting?
How was He stretching you? How was He preparing you?

2. What was God up to in your season of waiting? Was He
working in ways you wouldn't have believed, even if you
were told? If so, spill the details.

3. What promises from the Bible did you see play out in your everyday life during this time?

Our final step in this chapter is to spend some time with Allyson Golden. She's ready to encourage us by sharing how she has seen God work in her own season of waiting and leave us with practical tips we can apply to our lives today.

a purposeful chat
with Allyson Golden

"The waiting is worth it when we are waiting on the Lord. We don't have to see it or feel it to know God is working. He hasn't left you. He hasn't paused. He hasn't taken a break. He is doing something only He can do in this very moment."

Allyson Golden

HOPE: Tell us about a season of waiting that you've walked through in your life.

ALLYSON: For over a year, I wrestled with feeling like it was time to quit my job as a full-time nurse. I had felt the Lord calling me to pursue writing and ministry full time, but I wasn't sure how this was going to play out. This was probably the biggest season of waiting that I've ever walked through.

I waited and waited for His direction. This was especially hard because I felt so burned out in my nursing career and really wanted to speed up getting to a place where I could write and pursue ministry.

After sitting in this season for a full year, I felt the Lord finally telling me to quit my job. So I said to Him, "Okay, Lord. You told me to quit, so I'm going to trust You to provide financially."

I gave my employers a two months' notice and felt the Lord calling me to fast to get clarity and direction from Him.

You'll never guess what happened the next day at work.

My manager offered for me to work six shifts a month, which is one to two days a week like I had been dreaming of working. The Lord had made a way when I literally thought this schedule was an impossible dream.

This new part-time position allows me to help people in the hospital while also putting energy into the new passions and desires that God has placed on my heart.

HOPE: What has God taught you through the waiting?

ALLYSON: We are always in a waiting season for something. I'm in a new season of waiting today, and I'm sure as soon as this season ends, I'll be in another. The enemy wants us to feel confused and to believe God isn't doing anything, when that is not the case. I thought my life was going to be so much better if I could just leave my nursing position. God taught me that His plan is so much better than anything we would plan for ourselves.

HOPE: How will you walk through your next season of waiting?

ALLYSON: I am trying to silence distractions in my life, so I'm fasting from social media. This isn't going to speed up the waiting season, but it will allow me to seek the Lord with all my heart.

I'm spending time in prayer with God and laying this season at His feet. I have asked Him to help me see what He is doing around me. He is continuing to teach me that His plan will be better than I could have ever imagined.

HOPE: **What advice do you have for the girl who is in the middle of a season of waiting today?**

ALLYSON: The evidence of God is everywhere when you start to look for it. Take time to see what the Lord is doing in your life today. God does not withhold good things from those who are walking uprightly with Him (Psalm 84:11). He is preparing you for the great gift that He has for you. Ask Him to align your heart desires with His. Ask Him to give you the strength in this waiting season. Ask Him to uphold you through what may feel like a storm. He is with you. He is leading you. His plans and purpose for your life will exceed anything you could have ever asked for or even imagined on your own (Ephesians 3:20).

As Allyson tells us, it's important to remember that *you* are chosen. You are deeply loved, and there is so much purpose in the moment that is right in front of you.

How can you seek to find purpose in the moment? What steps can you take to remember that you are chosen and loved in your season of waiting?

when you are called out of your comfort zone

> *"I could not help but think that somewhere along the way we had missed what is radical about our faith and replaced it with what is comfortable."*[1]
>
> **David Platt**

What if you dared to take a courageous leap of faith to where God is calling you today? What if you made a choice to go for it and never look back?

The confusion that comes with the internal conflict of saying *yes* or *no* is hard to navigate, isn't it? Truth be told, there is a little more to the Pepperdine story than learning some anonymous donors had given me a scholarship eight days before student orientation. This opportunity didn't just change my perspective on how God works in the waiting. It also changed my perspective on how God shows up outside of our comfort zones.

Would you believe me if I told you that I almost said no to this opportunity? The truth is, moving to Malibu scared me.

I'd grown up in a sweet little town called Greenwood, Arkansas. With just 10,000 residents, it's one of those communities where everyone knows everyone and most choose to stay nearby for the long haul. This was all I had ever known.

On top of this, I had never even visited Pepperdine's campus and had been to California only once when I was a child. My high school best friend was going to be my roommate at Arkansas Tech, and my high school boyfriend would be there too. How was I supposed to shift my plans to attend college 1,560 miles away from home in a place where I didn't know a soul and had never even visited?

This entire situation felt crazy, but it was so clear that God had made a way for this to be possible. I was going to have to put my faith above my fear.

We've both been here, haven't we? We can see where God is calling us, but we're paralyzed by fear. We don't know exactly what He is doing or how He is going to do it. We want to go for it and know we should go for it, but there is still something terrifying that comes with saying yes.

I'll never forget the conversation my dad and I had. He said something to the tune of this: "Hope, you need to make a decision you won't regret when you're fifty." He went on to say, "What's the worst that can happen? You try it. It doesn't work out. We figure it out."

The decision felt life altering, and it was, but knowing that my dad was there to catch me if I fell comforted me.

The next eight days played out differently than expected, to say the least. My best friend decided she no longer wanted to be friends with me, and my boyfriend broke up with me. I had never imagined that a yes from Pepperdine would lead to a no from these two important people in my life at the time.

I really couldn't do much other than trust that God had moved what felt like mountains to make Pepperdine possible, so surely He had a greater plan in store.

My parents and I boarded a flight to LAX with my three suitcases, and the journey started.

Before I knew it, Pepperdine became my home away from home. This one yes served as a launching pad for many other yeses that would follow. Looking back, I can't imagine life without this yes.

When you look back at your life, can you see how one step of faith led you to where you are now? If your answer is yes, but you still struggle to say yes to that one thing that's tugging at your heart strings today, you're not alone. Taking a leap of faith doesn't ever get easier or less confusing, does it?

Getting called out of our comfort zones can present itself in different ways. Sometimes God calls us out of our comfort zones exactly where we are. Sometimes stepping out of our comfort zones is saying no so we can make room for a yes.

After months of asking why the logistics hadn't worked out for me to take a full-time ministry job, I realized that God was calling me to share my faith at the job I was already in.

But what in the world would this look like? How would people respond? What if I got fired for offending someone?

If anyone at work asked me about my weekend, I'd always casually slip in that we went to church, but that was pretty much the extent of bringing up my faith in the workplace. So why was God calling me to minister in the very place I wanted to run away from? I finally understood how Jonah must have felt when he ran away from God and landed in the belly of the whale (Jonah 1).

Like Jonah, I wanted to hide from God and ignore the call He was placing on my life. Instead, I asked God on the way to work to tell me where and how He wanted me to show up today.

This trust in Him led me on a powerful journey.

There were days when I'd resist His mission because I felt too uncomfortable. But there were also days when I really allowed God to use me at work. Some days it looked like being a listening ear to a colleague; other days it meant responding to a situation in the exact opposite of how I wanted to. Some days this looked like inviting girls from work to a coffee shop and sharing a verse or something God was teaching me. Other days this looked like finding time to silently pray for those in my department. Some days this looked like not understanding why things were going the way they were and surrendering to God. Other days this looked like seeing the bigger picture of what God was doing even when my circumstances would lead me to believe otherwise.

Sometimes stepping out of our comfort zones is saying no so we can make room for a yes.

What if stepping outside of our comfort zones isn't reserved for big, bold moments? What if we're all being offered a daily invitation to live mission-driven lives with God? What if that place that feels purposeless is actually full of opportunities to live out what He has called us to? If He has provided for us in those big moments before, won't He be faithful to provide for us in those moments that may seem small and unnoticeable?

Today, you're on a journey to discover how you can live a life outside of your comfort zone and say yes to the everyday, ordinary moments with Him. This is going to be a yes that you'll look back on and, as my father said, "won't regret when you're fifty."

In this chapter, we'll learn to:

- spend time reflecting on what God has done to lead you exactly where He has placed you today
- dig into the mission that God has defined for each of us
- identify practical ways that we can give Him our yes and live with a purpose that doesn't pause

We'll then revisit our friend Maddee Hill. She'll share her story of how God was calling her on a path that didn't lead to college and how she lives her life today, even when it still doesn't come natural to her.

outside of the status quo

Grab a pen, play "Oceans (Where Feet May Fail)" by Hillsong United, and let's dive into these questions.

1. When was a time that you felt called out of your comfort zone? Describe the situation and how this felt.

2. What decision did you make? What was the hardest or most confusing part of making the decision?

3. What did God teach you during this situation?

4. How does life look different today because of that decision?

5. Do you feel like you are living out your purpose today? Why, or why not?

6. In what ways is God calling you to step outside of your comfort zone where He has placed you today?

7. Write three small steps you could take to live purposefully today, and use this space to share those with God in prayer.

living on a mission

What would life look like if we lived as if we were on a mission? What if we said yes every day to something bigger than ourselves? How different would daily life feel if we felt connected to our ultimate purpose?

I recently had the opportunity to interview for a promotion. A mentor gave me this tip: "Before you go into the interview, decide how you want to be remembered and how you'd tackle the job. Once you've decided that, step into the interview intentionally and answer every question with that in mind."

This advice took away the pressure to perform in a way that I thought the interviewers expected. I didn't have to spend time guessing what they might be thinking or trying to say what they wanted to hear. Instead, I walked in knowing who I was and how I wanted to attack the role. Using this approach, I was able to enter the interview with a level of focus, intentionality, and confidence I'd never felt before.

We can all apply this approach to our daily lives. Even when we don't know what we're walking into each day, we don't have to walk into it purposelessly. We can rely on knowing who God says we are and what God says our purpose is. That truth can give us the focus, intentionality, and confidence to face any situation.

> If God has provided for us in those big moments before, won't He be faithful to provide for us in those moments that may seem small and unnoticeable?

What if we went into each day knowing who we are and what we're about? What if we intentionally took the time to center ourselves on this before we walked into each day?

This way of living allows us to joyfully take each step as a child of God who is on a mission. This purpose-driven mission is straightforward when we really think about it. As we've acknowledged, the Bible tells us we are called to love God and love the people around us. How different would it feel if we strategically and confidently approached each day with this mission?

God doesn't ask us to go on this mission alone. When we feel alone, we can trust and know that we can do this through Him alone. Psalm 23:4 says, "Even though I walk through the darkest valley, I will fear no evil, for you are with me; your rod and your staff, they comfort me."

See? Even the darkest places and spaces don't have to be so scary. We can find comfort when we invite Him into our walks. Places that feel pointless are actually purposeful when we step into living as the people He has called us to be.

Philippians 4:12–13 says, "I know what it is to be in need, and I know what it is to have plenty. I have learned the secret of being content in any and every situation, whether well fed or hungry, whether living in plenty or in want. I can do all this through him who gives me strength."

We can rely on knowing who God says we are and what God says our purpose is. That truth can give us the focus, intentionality, and confidence to face any situation.

This verse becomes especially powerful when we realize Paul wrote this while he was in prison for living out the mission and the purpose God gave him. The same mission and purpose God gave to each one of us. Even when facing opposition and resistance that most of us can't imagine, Paul found the hope, peace, and joy that are promised to all of us.

Leading up to this verse, Paul said, "Rejoice in the Lord always. I will say it again: Rejoice! Let your gentleness be evident to all. The Lord is near. Do not be anxious about anything, but in every situation, by prayer and petition, with thanksgiving, present your requests to God. And the peace of God, which transcends all understanding, will guard your hearts and your minds in Christ Jesus" (Philippians 4:4–7).

the daily yes

We don't have to know every single detail of the yes. We don't have to have it all figured out before choosing to step into it. All we have to do is show up where God has placed us. It may feel small and at times insignificant, but He can do things we wouldn't imagine with each step of obedience we take.

Shortly after saying yes to sharing my faith at work, God placed it on my heart to start a casual Bible study with some female coworkers. This felt really intimidating. While I knew some of the women on a professional basis, there was one girl I'd only met over Zoom.

Guess what happened? The same day I made the decision that I'd do it, I ran into this girl! Isn't that so like God to give us a little wink of confidence when we feel like we're taking a step that is out of our comfort zones?

Our group began meeting at a little local coffee shop close to our office. Sometimes one girl would show up. Other days, three. But this yes ended up leading to something I never would have expected.

It started with the coffee shop being crowded. I'll never forget showing up and seeing two of the girls from the group sitting at an eight-person table. At the opposite end of the table, a beautiful blonde was working at her laptop. We didn't know her, so those old fears resurfaced in me. What if we offend this girl? What if she's annoyed that we're having a Bible study while she's trying to work?

> All we have to do is show up
> where God has placed us.

There weren't any open seats to move to, so I decided to just dive in with the message placed on my heart that day. We talked about Jeremiah and how even after years of preaching, he still questioned what God was calling him to do. God told him in Jeremiah 1:5, "Before I formed you in the womb I knew you, before you were born I set you apart; I appointed you as a prophet to the nations."

Jeremiah responded with excuses, insisting that he didn't know how to speak and that he was too young to be a prophet (Jeremiah 1:6).

Jeremiah 1:7–8 shows us God's response: "Do not say, 'I am too young.' You must go to everyone I send you to and say whatever I command you. Do not be afraid of them, for I am with you and will rescue you,' declares the LORD."

Little did I know when preparing this message that I'd be questioning my purpose and qualifications just like Jeremiah had done. Sure enough, God's faithfulness started playing out in front of my eyes in a way I least expected.

When we don't know what we are doing, God is faithful to show us what He is doing. When the girls and I finished the message, we started catching up on life and sharing prayer requests. Then I shared that I was pregnant, and another girl in the group told us she was too. That is when something surprising happened.

The girl at the end of the table stood up and smiled. She said something like, "I can't help but say something. I'm pregnant too!"

She had the cutest bump, and she explained that she'd just moved to the community for her husband's job. She asked about the Bible study, and we exchanged numbers. The next time the Bible study met, she was the only girl who showed up. We were able to talk about our faith, and she shared that she was on a journey to reconnect with God.

Isn't this so like God? We think we're saying yes to one thing and He totally blows our minds when He gives us a little sneak peek of what He is actually up to. He takes the yes we finally warm up to and uses that yes to show us how faithful, powerful, and incredible He is. He takes our small steps and makes big moves.

So, we've made the decision that we want to give God our yes and go into each day with a purpose that doesn't pause, but how do we make this happen? Here are some action steps we can take together starting today:

1. Identify the places and spaces that God has you in today.
2. Write out how you can show up in each of these places today. Identify what feels purposeless and what could hold you back some days from saying yes to this way of living.
3. Figure out a way to remind yourself of who you are and the mission you're on each day.
4. Write out how you want to start intentionally living with this mindset and mission.
5. Invite God into each day. Ask Him to show you where He is leading you, to give you comfort and peace that only come from Him, and to position you where He planned before you were even born.
6. Watch for Him to show up. Each day write down a step you took that you're proud of. Note how you see God working in your life.

**God takes our small steps
and makes big moves.**

Here's some space for you to monitor your progress this week and track some of your wins:

Now let's hear how Maddee Hill learned to go where God is leading.

a purposeful chat
with Maddee Hill

"You can't force it if it isn't God's plan, and you can't stop it if it is! There has to come a point where you surrender your plan because the one that He has for you is so much better and so much bigger than you think."

Maddee Hill

HOPE: When is a time that you felt like God called you out of your comfort zone?

MADDEE: All the best things in my life have happened outside of my comfort zone. One of the biggest, most challenging examples to date is the decision to not go to college. I loved the social life and wanted to be with my friends. But during my senior year, I would tour colleges and leave with the worst feeling after each visit. You know when something just doesn't feel right?

Each visit felt more and more like the Lord wasn't calling me to college. I can't explain it other than I just didn't have peace. I remember after each visit my parents asking me what I thought, and I'd already be on the verge of tears. I really wanted college to be right for me. I'm so thankful that my parents took time to listen and support me.

It soon became clear that college might not be what I was supposed to be doing. This was really hard because everyone around me was going to college. I felt like I would be failing if I chose not to go.

I decided to table the idea and take a gap year. During this gap year, I would intern at my church while figuring out if college was totally out of the picture or not.

HOPE: What was the hardest part of stepping into what God was calling you to?

MADDEE: The hardest thing for me was having to tell other people. I absolutely dreaded people asking me why. I knew not everyone was going to be supportive. Sure enough, the blank stares happened. Most didn't know how to respond. It wasn't the path they were expecting for me. I'll never forget my senior night as a volleyball player. My graduating class had about 1,200 students, and the attendance at our games was high.

My parents were on both sides of me as they walked me into the middle of the court. The announcer was introducing each senior on the team and telling the crowd what college we'd be attending and what we planned to study. You can probably imagine how this was going to go for me. As my parents walked with me, the announcer said something like "Here is Maddee Hill. She is going to … She's actually going into ministry."

He literally stuttered during my announcement. The entire gym was practically silent. I was the only girl on the entire team not going to college.

HOPE: **How did you step out of your comfort zone and into where God was calling you?**

MADDEE: During the internship at my church, I felt this stirring and just knew God was doing something in my heart. He placed people in my life who called out the gifts that He had given me— even when I couldn't necessarily see the gifts myself. Over time it became clear that He had given me a heart for people, specifically for people who were lost and didn't know Him.

The people who knew me best were able to help me navigate this time. My parents played a large role, and my church's host team pastor, Cindy, started to pull those gifts out of me. She encouraged me to think about making ministry my career.

At this point in time, it still really scared me to do something that no one else was doing. I was crippled by the thought of others thinking I was weird.

I decided to completely surrender this situation to Him. I remember saying, "I'm confused, but I trust You." This became a daily prayer for me as I surrendered this decision to Him.

HOPE: **What did you end up deciding to do?**

MADDEE: The internship was coming to an end, and it was time to decide if I wanted to apply for a six-month internship, which would be the final step before going full time at my church. Cindy suggested that I apply, and I knew she was right. I was still fearful, but this time, I had peace in the fear. It felt way different from the fear when I had visited different colleges with my parents.

After the first internship came to an end, I interviewed for the full-time internship and got it. Six months later, I was officially on staff doing full-time ministry at my church.

HOPE: What did God teach you during this season?

MADDEE: Even though there were times when I would question if full-time ministry was really the calling God had on my life, I somehow found confidence in it. I didn't think I would have been hired if this wasn't the door that He'd planned for me to walk through.

Looking back, the enemy knew the doubts that were inside my head, and impostor syndrome hit a bit. I would think, *Did they pick the right girl? Am I called to this? Is this actually what the Lord wants me to do?*

God taught me that He doesn't call the equipped; He equips the called. God won't call us to something and then leave us high and dry. Knowing that God was going to sustain me really helped me break through my biggest fears and doubts.

HOPE: Do you ever feel scared to step out of your comfort zone today? If so, how do you break free from those fears now?

MADDEE: Remember how Cindy showed me my gifts and encouraged me to go into ministry full time? Today, I'm getting to do the same role she does, host team pastor, at another church campus. It feels like a full-circle moment to get to lead in this capacity and inspire people the way Cindy inspired me.

As far as feeling outside of my comfort zone today, sometimes my age causes me to doubt where God has me. This has been the biggest hurdle for me.

Just as I had to surrender the idea of going to college to the Lord and lean on Him to direct my steps, I have to constantly give the doubts over to Him today. Honestly, being out of my comfort zone is a weekly thing. Over and over again, I say, "Lord, I cannot do this by myself."

It doesn't come natural to me to have confidence in leading people who are older and more experienced than me. Once again, I catch myself questioning if they picked the right girl. That's when I pray: "I know You placed me here. I know there is purpose here, and I know You are going to do it through me. Give me the wisdom to do it."

Whenever I start to feel insecure, I remember this verse: "Don't let anyone look down on you because you are young, but set an example for the believers in speech, in conduct, in love, in faith and in purity" (1 Timothy 4:12).

HOPE: **What would you tell the girl who is walking through this season?**

MADDEE: I would tell you not everyone will understand, and that is okay. Whenever the opinions of others feel stifling, remind yourself that you are doing none of this to please them. Keep your circle small when it comes to who you can trust. Make a choice to put your relationship with God first, and watch how He leads and comforts you when you're in uncomfortable places. Don't stop seeking the

Lord in it, especially when you feel vulnerable. Have the confidence that only comes from Him, and ask God to equip you with that each day regardless of what that situation looks like.

Maddee learned to trust in God to equip her, even when she felt too young or inexperienced for the job He was calling her to do.

What is an area of your life that you can trust God to equip you in? Use this space to write out a prayer, and invite God into this area of your life.

chapter 11 when you can't shake the opinion or approval of others

"What's the greater risk? Letting go of what people think or letting go of how I feel, what I believe, and who I am?"[1]

Brené Brown

Do you ever catch yourself worrying about what others think about you? Do you ever strive to gain the approval of others? Do you try to please the people around you? Do you ever question who you really are because you have been living for everyone else?

We're in the same boat if:

- making a decision looks more like taking a poll on what the people in your life think
- setting boundaries makes you feel guilty, but you will gladly honor boundaries set by other people
- putting a smile on your face and sucking it up is sometimes easier than being open and honest with those around you, especially when hard conversations need to happen
- letting go of criticism from others is hard to do and you catch yourself replaying what they said over and over in your head
- agreeing with what someone else says in a conversation is your go-to approach, even if you don't really feel that way
- thinking about upsetting someone causes you to worry before it has even happened, and enjoying the present moment is sometimes hard because you dread how you might upset someone in an upcoming situation
- explaining your identity sounds exactly like who others in your life want you to be, even if it's not true to you

A few years into post grad, these truths hit me. How were they not clear before? The first step was admitting this sad reality to my husband, Will.

I'd spent so much time living for the approval of others and striving to keep them happy no matter what it took that I wasn't even sure who I was.

There, I'd said it. I'd stated the obvious. Everyone knew I'd do anything to make them happy, and some had even taken advantage of it.

Do you ever ask yourself why you're doing what you're doing and who you're doing it for? If you have a hard time shaking the opinions and striving for the approval of others, the answer to this question may be a little alarming. In my case, the truth was, I was living my life exactly how others wanted me to, even if that meant completely abandoning my authentic self.

Each decision was carefully made to live up to the expectations of who I thought others wanted me to be. My entire life was programmed on a setting that was not only unrealistic but didn't align with how I knew God was calling me to live.

If making a decision looks more like taking an agenda item to a board meeting than doing what you feel called to do, we're in the same camp. If just the thought of making someone upset or disappointed gives you anxiety, I know how you feel.

> I'd spent so much time living for the approval of others and striving to keep them happy no matter what it took that I wasn't even sure who I was.

So, how did I finally recognize this unhealthy way of living at the age of twenty-six? I saw a significantly huge disconnect had formed between how I showed up for my professional life and how I lived my personal life. In one space, there was freedom. In the other, fear, insecurity, and striving.

At work, I had been leading teams of people and was responsible for large projects that impacted the company. Not only was I expected to make decisions on a daily basis, but I was also expected to do this quickly. The schedules allowed no time to pause and chase down the approval of others before giving a head nod or coming up with a plan. I had no time to run my own public-relations campaign to make sure everyone at work understood each decision and saw me in a positive light.

Sure, the first few times someone misunderstood me at work were difficult, but there was too much going on to fixate on it. I had to quickly get comfortable with making decisions that weren't always popular or understood. Decisions at work were made from the perspective of what my role was and what my responsibilities to the company were at that point in time.

This mindset simplified things, and suddenly an aha moment occurred. Even though Will and I had a house and bills by this point, my personal life had kept me living inside my familiar, self-created box labeled "people pleaser."

The thing is, people-pleasing takes a lot of work, and I already had a full-time job.

How could I be seen as a leader at work yet feel like a kid seeking approval when I stepped outside of the office? How had it gotten to the point where I wasn't even sure who I really was because I was still striving to be who I thought others wanted me to be? How different would life look and feel if I broke free from the one thing in my life that had constantly held me back?

If you don't really have a true answer when you ask yourself who you are, you aren't the only one who has felt that way. If your response to who you are today mirrors who you think others perceive you as or who you think others want you to be, don't be so hard on yourself. If you feel defeated just thinking about breaking free from what has guided you most of your life, I'm here to tell you there is life on the other side of this. We're going to do this together.

Keeping up with this way of life isn't sustainable. Our purpose can never be paused by the opinions and approvals of those around us. We just think it can.

What if there is another way? What if we can shake the opinions of others? What if their approval doesn't really carry the weight we once believed?

We're going to learn how we can press play in our everyday lives without looking to others for permission first. We don't have to chase down the approval of those around us when we realize that the One who created us already approves of us.

We're invited to do life guided by the One who remains the same yesterday, today, and tomorrow. Who He says we are and what He calls us to do not change. His agenda is clear—He wants to love us unconditionally and spend eternity with us at His side. He wants what is best for us, and that remains the consistent, everyday truth we can walk in.

Get ready to claim your freedom, friend. We're going to find it together as we learn to:

- reflect on the areas of our lives where we can't shake the opinion of others

- identify two steps we can take to break free from what others think and stop striving for the approval of those around us

We'll finish up with a word from Georgia Brown, who will share her personal experience with being held back by the opinions of others before learning to break free.

time to reflect

Before we dig into it, let's reflect on specific areas where we can't seem to shake the opinions of others. You know the drill. Grab a pen, play the song called "Keep Me in the Moment" by Jeremy Camp, and answer the questions below:

1. In what area of your life do you catch yourself seeking the opinion and approval of others? Why?

2. Reflect on a time when you struggled to make a decision without knowing what the people in your life thought. Share the details and what that experience was like.

3. How does trying to get approval from others make you feel? Where do you think this desire stems from? How long has this been a part of your life?

4. Whose approval in your life do you strive to keep? Whose opinions matter to you most?

5. Do you struggle with knowing who you really are? If you were to describe who you are, what would you say?

6. How do you think others would describe you? How do you try to live up to this in your daily life?

7. What do you think life would look and feel like if you were able to shake the opinions and approval of others? Have

you ever tried to do this before? If so, what went well and
what didn't?

8. Write two opinions that have stuck with you, and use this
space to hand those over to God in prayer.

step one: look up

Imagine that you arrive at your favorite coffee shop. You walk up to
the counter to place your order, and the barista tells you that a random customer wants you to order for them. How would you even
begin to know what they wanted? What are the odds that you'd
order something they liked? The probability of ordering them their
usual would be even lower, right? I don't know about you, but I
wouldn't want someone else guessing my coffee order if that were my
only shot at getting a cup of coffee that day.

In a way, this is how we treat the calling on our lives when we
look to others for guidance. Why do we trust them to navigate our
lives for us? Especially when the Bible clearly tells us that God will
lead us in the direction that is best for us? If we are aware that we
don't have insight into the assignments God has given to those

around us, why do we assume those around us somehow have the inside scoop?

We just might miss out on the full experience that God designed for us if we continue to give others power they were never intended to have.

This leads us to the first step we're going to take together. We're going to change where our eyes gaze and what our minds focus on when we are seeking wisdom, advice, and that stamp of approval. Colossians 3:2 says, "Set your minds on things above, not on earthly things."

Are you starting to see it? We've been called out and called up, friend. We are called to live in the world, not of the world. The answers and guidance we are looking for aren't going to be found around us. We'll gain the clarity and wisdom we've been searching for when we choose to look to God first and seek after Him. The Lord said in Jeremiah 29:13, "You will seek me and find me when you seek me with all your heart."

We're going to have to get comfortable with not always receiving a response that is as immediate as we want. We're going to have to be patient and trust that He is working and making moves on our behalf. We're going to have to spend time in His Word and intentionally carve out space to communicate with Him.

As Hebrews 11:1 says, "Now faith is confidence in what we hope for and assurance about what we do not see." (I encourage you to read Hebrews 11 to be reminded of God's faithfulness to His people.)

Over and over again in the Bible, we see fellow brothers and sisters in Christ go against what we can be sure other people were telling them to do. Instead of listening to others, they looked to the Lord for wisdom and approval. They stepped into His plan for them. Did it always make sense to them at the time? We can assume it probably didn't, but they trusted Him anyway. That same God who was with them is the same God who is with us.

Here are some ways you can "look up" in your daily life:

- Spend time in prayer asking for clarity and wisdom on the assignment God has for you.
- Write down the areas of your life in which you struggle to let go of the opinions and approval of others, and pray over them.
- Turn your worries and the weight of what others think into worship. As you're singing and praising God, invite Him into your day and ask Him to continue to transform your heart.
- Read the Bible and ask God to show you more about who He is and what He says about you. Tell Him that you want to keep growing in your faith and that you want to focus your eyes on Him alone.

step two: remind ourselves of our "why" when things feel shaky again

The second step we can take when we start to second-guess God's plan is to intentionally remind ourselves of our "why."

Is there an area of your life where you already know stepping away from people-pleasing is going to feel like an uphill battle? If so, you're not alone. As we've been chatting today, it became clear that there are a couple of areas of my own life where I still feel stifled by my tendency to seek approval.

While waiting to learn if I'd landed the promotion, I was already worried about what my peers would think if it worked out for me. Would they be upset that I'd been promoted? Would they think I didn't deserve the new role? Would they be offended that I hadn't told them I was applying for the position? Would they feel like this situation was unfair to them?

This is where we have to intentionally remind ourselves of our "why." We can't choose to avoid going through an open door just because of what people might say behind closed doors. We can't choose to not take that step just because someone might disapprove of our choices.

Let's reflect on the following questions to help us understand our "why" again:

- Did we pray about the decision before we made it?
- Do we trust that God is faithful to His people and keeps His promises?
- Are we trying to please the people around us or the One who created us?
- Will people have opinions regardless of what direction the Lord leads us in?
- Do the opinions and approval of others have to carry the same weight in our lives as they used to?
- Who does God say we are?
- What does God call us to do?

Once we've reflected and recentered, we can find encouragement from God's Word to navigate it all. Here are some verses that can help us as we make a daily decision to follow His lead, shake off the opinions of others, and stop striving for approval outside of Him:

- When our hearts are torn between where we've been and how we're going to live moving forward, we can focus on this verse: "Whatever you do, work at it with all your heart, as working for the Lord, not for human masters, since you know that you will receive an inheritance from the Lord as a reward. It is the Lord Christ you are serving" (Colossians 3:23–24).

- When we catch ourselves trying to gain the approval of others, we can focus on this verse: "Am I now trying to win the approval of human beings, or of God? Or am I trying to please people? If I were still trying to please people, I would not be a servant of Christ" (Galatians 1:10).

- When we start to worry about the happiness of those around us and what they are really thinking about us, we can focus on this verse: "Do not be anxious about anything, but in every situation, by prayer and petition, with thanksgiving, present your requests to God" (Philippians 4:6).

- When we think it would be easier to go back to our people-pleasing ways, we can focus on this verse: "Do not be conformed to this world, but be transformed by the renewal of your mind, that by testing you may discern what is the will of God, what is good and acceptable and perfect" (Romans 12:2 ESV).

- When we feel like the opinions and approval of others are going to impact our lives, we can focus on this verse: "Fear of man will prove to be a snare, but whoever trusts in the LORD is kept safe" (Proverbs 29:25).

- When we begin to second-guess the calling on our lives and are tempted to find security in the opinions of others, we can focus on this verse: "It is better to take refuge in the LORD than to trust in humans" (Psalm 118:8).

Look at how far we've come in just a few pages. Feel free to meet me back here as often as you'd like. Next up, let's meet Georgia Brown, who will remind us of the power of words.

a purposeful chat
with Georgia Brown

"Maybe you, too, have been carrying the weight of someone's words. Reality is, we may not always have the chance to tell that person how their words made us feel, but we can ALWAYS bring them to our Father, who doesn't only listen but also heals, restores, and renews His children's spirits."

Georgia Brown

HOPE: Tell us why you are so passionate about the power our words can have.

GEORGIA: I don't think we realize the power our words hold. God's Word makes it clear that the power of the tongue is life and death (Proverbs 18:21). We can choose to speak in a way that creates life or in a way that creates death. One way points us up, and one points us down.

Every moment, we really have to guard our words. Before we even realize it, we can catch ourselves struggling with insecurity, self-doubt, and body image. But in most cases, these seeds of insecurity were planted with words.

HOPE: How would you describe what it feels like to be held back by the opinions of others? Tell us about an experience from your life.

GEORGIA: Let's take this analogy of seeds further. I tend to look at the heart like a garden. If you look at your heart this way and the things people have said to you, you can picture their words as either flowers or weeds. In that same garden, your words are seeds too. You can choose to plant either flowers or weeds.

Here is what is sneaky, though. Sometimes weeds look like flowers, so you leave them in your garden and you let them grow. Before you know it, the weeds entangle themselves with the flowers and start to blend right in. Your good flowers start losing their nutrients because the weeds are stealing from them. The weeds can be uprooted, but the longer they are in there, the stronger their roots become. It hurts more to uproot them later down the road.

Let's add a personal touch to this analogy. Someone who isn't in your inner circle might say something that doesn't really hurt you all that much. But it's a much different hurt when those same words come from one of your loved ones.

For so long, I didn't realize that words from my brother were getting to me. We're best friends and even live together as roommates. We love each other. A lot. But he was still seeing me as who I was before I gave my whole life to Jesus. It really hurt because he would poke at me with his words, trying to bring up my past.

I finally broke down and started thinking, *What if these tears I've been holding back are exactly what God wants to use to water the garden of my heart?*

The first step that helped me was allowing myself to face my pain and cry those tears. Then I had a hard conversation with my brother, letting him know how his opinions had hurt me.

HOPE: How do you break free from the opinions of others?

GEORGIA: We can turn to other people all day long, but the only thing that is really going to change us is going to God and reading His Word. Let's ask ourselves: How many weeds are in our garden? How many opinions that simply aren't true have we allowed to become parts of our identity?

This may look like a parent telling you that you are never going to be good enough. Or maybe it is the world telling you that you need to be a size zero. Or maybe it's someone assuming you're still the person you were in the past. When we make the choice to no longer view other people's opinions as truth, we are uprooting the weeds that are entangled in our hearts.

Of course, once we uproot those weeds, our final step is to fill that space with Scripture, encouragement, and God's truth.

HOPE: What would you say to the girl who is surrounded by words that aren't life-giving?

GEORGIA: I've heard it said that you become a combination of the five people you are around the most. I encourage you to look closely at who is getting most of your time. If your work environment is hard or if your family environment is tricky, how can you prioritize spending time with God and putting Him first in your daily life?

Matthew 6:33 says, "But seek first his kingdom and his righteousness, and all these things will be given to you as well." When we seek His kingdom first and spend time with Him, we have a firm foundation. This gives us a renewed focus that allows us to be centered and grounded in any situation.

This also allows us not to let anyone steal our peace. The only way that we can walk in peace is if we spend time doing life with the One who is peace. He wants us to surrender it all. Maybe for you this looks like giving your burdens at work to Him, or maybe it's handing over the problems within your family or your marital struggles or the issues within your friend group. Whatever it may be, the only way that we can become our best selves is if God gets all of us.

HOPE: Is there any advice you have for the girl trying to decipher who she should allow into her life and who she shouldn't?

GEORGIA: Luke 6:45 says, "A good man brings good things out of the good stored up in his heart, and an evil man brings evil things out of the evil stored up in his heart. For the mouth speaks what the heart is full of." This reveals that our words and the words of those around us are an overflow of the heart.

Anytime anyone opens their mouth, you are getting a glimpse into the journal of their heart. Pay close attention to what people say. This will allow you to decide how to handle their opinions and the words they speak over your life.

I love how Georgia talks about looking at the heart like a garden. What words are you holding on to that have planted flowers in your heart? What words are you holding on to that have planted weeds in your heart? How can you uproot the weeds?

Let's take it one step further. How can you plant seeds of flowers in the hearts of others?

what if we are free from what once held us back?

> *"God never promises to remove us from our struggles. He does promise, however, to change the way we look at them."*[1]
>
> **Max Lucado**

As we come to the end of this journey, are you able to look back and see just how much progress you've made with God by your side? Do you see evidence of how God has carried you and equipped you in this season? Can you see that your PURPOSE DOESN'T PAUSE?

The work we did in these pages wasn't always easy, but we didn't avoid the resistance, trials, or confusion that we encountered.

We've given it our all and tackled some of the most painful, discouraging, and stifling parts of our lives. We've broken chains and found freedom that we didn't even know existed. We've stepped into our purpose, which we can confidently say was never on pause. We've found life at what felt like a dead end.

Confusion no longer has a hold on us. Now we can see that we were never stuck; we just thought we were. We've accepted an invitation to show up daily, love God with all our heart, and love the people He places around us.

Now, here's what we're going to do next:

- Reflect on how far we've come in our personal journey to discover our purpose that doesn't pause. This will allow us to celebrate the freedom we've found where life used to hold us back.
- Identify one truth from each of the places we visited together in chapters 2–11. These ten takeaways will be like souvenirs we can carry with us in our everyday lives.
- Spend time reading over some final words of encouragement before we have to say "see you soon!"

look how far you've come!

There is something so neat about reflecting back on where we started and looking at the progress we've made. We're reminded of God's faithfulness to keep His promises to us. And we see that He was always at work in ways we wouldn't have believed, even if we'd been told.

Go ahead and play the song "On Our Way" by MercyMe, and let's do a progress check-in.

1. How did this journey start for you? How would you describe where you are today?

2. What did you think your purpose was when you opened these pages? How do you view your purpose today?

3. Where did you feel stuck and held back at the beginning of our journey? What have you been able to break free from?

4. How did you face resistance when we started? How are you going to face trials and confusion when they greet you in the future?

As we reflect on this final question and prayer prompt, play the song "Evidence" by Josh Baldwin.

5. What wins and progress have you seen in your life when you look back?

6. Write three things God has taught you through this journey, and use this space to share these with God in prayer.

ten takeaways to carry with us

As we discussed at the beginning of this journey, I want you to feel free to come back to these pages as often as you'd like. God has brought you to this book for a reason. You belong here!

Until we come back together again, let me leave you with this final list of ten key takeaways. You can carry these truths with you wherever God takes you next.

> **When you're questioning why you are where you are, remember this:**
> God can use what you see as a setback to set you up for what He is calling you to right now. The same God who has carried you your entire life is with you and for you each and every day.

When your dreams aren't what you pictured, remember this:

You're invited to step outside of the box you've placed yourself in and step into the very life that God designed for you. Your unmet expectations might just be unexpected gifts that He kindly gave to you.

When something good comes to an end, remember this:

You may not always know the next step or where your trials are leading you, but you get to walk with the One who is leading you. You don't have to carry the heavy load of knowing all that is ahead. You can embrace and live an abundant life today because your future is greater than your temporary struggles. The good that has come to an end in your life will all work together for His good (Romans 8:28).

When you don't feel loved or good enough, remember this:

Grace is the ultimate unexpected gift that God gives you and that was made possible through Jesus' death on the cross. It is His way of saving you when you inevitably fall short. Grace is how He extends His gift of forgiveness and love. Grace is God choosing you and seeing you as loved and worthy no matter what.

When you feel the pressure to figure out who you are, remember this:

Maybe the discontentment or confusion around who you are is just the start of becoming who God made you to be. When you embrace the identity that He gives you, your life begins to look different. Suddenly, life looks more like surrendering your everyday to Him and seeking Him as you take each step. It is a different type of action. It is a whole lot less pressure and a whole lot more fulfilling.

When you catch yourself struggling with comparison, remember this:

God is not limited by the limitations and gaps that comparison points out. He isn't stifled by how you thought life would look and how it is actually playing out for you. He doesn't look to see where you are in relation to His other children. He looks at you and sees you exactly where He intentionally placed you for a moment like this.

When your life feels out of control, remember this:

You don't have to continue feeling like you are free-falling. You are invited to walk freely with Him down the unshakable, purpose-filled path that He designed for you and is in control over.

When you are in a season of waiting, remember this:

Before you were born, God intricately and intentionally prepared a plan that was full of purpose for your life. This plan isn't suddenly put on hold or thrown out the door when you enter a season of waiting. When you feel frustrated, stuck, disappointed, forgotten, or anxious, God is working in ways you can't always see, feel, or understand. He opens doors that only He can open in His perfect timing. His ways don't always follow a step one, two, and three pattern that logically makes sense to you here on earth. His ways are higher and mightier than anything you could dream or possibly imagine.

When you are called out of your comfort zone, remember this:

Even when you don't know what you're walking into each day, you don't have to walk into it purposelessly. You can trust in who God says you are and what God says your purpose is.

When you can't shake the opinions or approval of others, remember this:

You don't have to continue living for other people's opinions or approval anymore. You're invited to do life guided by the One who remains the same yesterday, today, and tomorrow. Who He says you are and what He calls you to do not change. His agenda is loving you and spending eternity with you. He wants what is best for you, and that remains the consistent, everyday truth you can walk in.

encouragement for you

After writing that first book for DaySpring, I knew I had a second one in me. For more than a year, I prayed for God to give me clarity on what the message for this book was supposed to be. I got a little bold with my prayer and asked Him to break my heart for what breaks His. I bet you already know what He revealed: confusion, feeling stuck, and living life like my purpose was on pause.

Let's imagine being placed in a room with the lock on the outside of the door. Someone stops by and unlocks this door, but you've already come to believe it's locked. So, you keep sitting there, missing out on what's on the other side purely because of what you still consider to be true.

Are you starting to see a visualization of the work we just walked through come to life? Our generation of women will no longer be held back by chains we have already broken free from. We aren't going to be frozen in place by false beliefs and confusion. We have discovered the ultimate truth found in God's Word. We now know the door is unlocked. There is freedom on the other side. And it is ours.

In 1 Timothy 2:4–7, we read:

> He wants not only us but everyone saved, you know, everyone to get to know the truth we've learned: that there's one God and only one, and

one Priest-Mediator between God and us—Jesus, who offered himself in exchange for everyone held captive by sin, to set them all free. Eventually the news is going to get out. This and this only has been my appointed work: getting this news to those who have never heard of God, and explaining how it works by simple faith and plain truth. (MSG)

This is the truth that sets us free from the very things that have been holding us back. When we seek Him first, life starts to look different. Suddenly, our perspective changes. Our posture shifts. Our hearts are transformed. What was once important doesn't have the same hold on us anymore.

> Our generation of women will no longer be held back by chains we have already broken free from. We aren't going to be frozen in place by false beliefs and confusion.

As Ephesians 2:7–10 tells us:

Now God has us where he wants us, with all the time in this world and the next to shower grace and kindness upon us in Christ Jesus. Saving is all his idea, and all his work. All we do is trust him enough to let him do it. It's God's gift from start to finish! We don't play the major role. If we did, we'd probably go around bragging that we'd done

the whole thing! No, we neither make nor save ourselves. God does both the making and saving. He
creates each of us by Christ Jesus to join him in the
work he does, the good work he has gotten ready
for us to do, work we had better be doing. (MSG)

send-off prayer

Before we say "see you soon," I want to pray a send-off prayer over you:

Dear God,

Thank You for the girl who is reading this. We know that before
she was even created by You that You prepared a future for her. You
knew what she'd be walking into each day before the day even came.
You went ahead of her and paved the very path that she is walking
down today. It was You, God, who chose her, set her apart, and called
her to the life that she is living today.

I pray that when she starts to question who she is and what she
is doing, You'll gently remind her that You don't have any questions
when You look at her. You see her exactly as You created her to be—
as Your child, a child You love endlessly.

When she starts to feel like her life is on pause, show her evidence of how You are at work and moving where she is. When
confusion greets her again, give her peace that surpasses her understanding. When the days feel long and the season appears to be never
ending, cover her in Your love that never ceases. When she feels like
she is right back where she started, remind her that You made a way
when there was no way. When life feels like it's over, remind her that
each day here is one day closer to stepping into eternal life with You.

Show her how You want to use her where she is today. Give her strength when the assignment feels heavy and she's running out of energy. Give her joy when it's taking everything in her to put a smile on her face. Give her wisdom when she isn't sure what she is supposed to be doing or what decision she needs to make. Give her a light that she can carry into dark places and that cannot be blown out by the trials and sufferings she'll face. Give her love to carry into the lives of those who may have never experienced it before. Give her peace when she can't see what You are doing.

I pray that she shows up daily rooted in Your truth. I pray that she accepts Your invitation and chooses to do life with You in the small moments, the big moments, and the in-between moments. I pray that she sets her gaze on You and finds You when she seeks You. I pray that she never forgets that her PURPOSE DOESN'T PAUSE. In Jesus' name, amen.

see you soon!

The time has come. We're going to boldly run into the places and spaces that God put us in like we're on a mission. When the resistance, opposition, and suffering hit, what are we going to do? We're going to give it our all and remember that our PURPOSE DOESN'T PAUSE. We aren't going to sit around and wait for a different life because we know He has placed us exactly where He wants us today.

The fact that our paths crossed means more than you know. I can only imagine what God is going to continue to do within you and through you. He has prepared you for this exact moment. He has promoted you to the very position you find yourself in today. None of this was by mistake.

As Matthew 6:34 says, "Give your entire attention to what God is doing right now, and don't get worked up about what may or may not happen tomorrow. God will help you deal with whatever hard things come up when the time comes" (MSG).

Embrace what He is doing. Keep seeking after Him and His truth. Be expectant that He is doing things in your life that you wouldn't believe, even if you were told.

He's with you, friend. He's not leaving you now and He never has left you.

As our time comes to a close, I have one request for you. Since our lives are intertwined now, you're going to have to keep me updated on what God is doing in your life. Nothing would make me smile bigger than to hear from you and keep up with you. I'm so proud of how far we've come together and wouldn't have wanted to do this journey with anyone else.

See you soon!

●　●　●　●　●

As my special gift to you, I've created bonus
video content that you can access here:

Link: DavidCCook.org/access
Access code: Purpose

acknowledgments

This book wouldn't be in your hands if it weren't for these people in my life.

Will, thank you for the sacrifices you made to create the time and space that brought this book to life. Your encouragement carried me through it all. You are my rock and my safe place to land all in one. I couldn't imagine life with you!

Mom and Dad, thank you for teaching me about Jesus and pointing me to Him all of my days. I hope you read the stories about our journey together in these pages and smile. Your love for God and the prayers you've prayed over me have truly changed my life. I wouldn't be who I am without the two of you!

Janis and Allen, thank you for the countless dinners and encouraging me as this book was being written. You'll never know what your support and listening ear mean to me. I truly hit the in-law jackpot with the two of you!

Hannah, thank you for always being just a call away and helping me process my ideas. Our chats gave me the clarity and confidence to keep going. You're the best sister anyone could ask for!

Debbie, thank you for leaning into the calling God had on your life in this season. Without you, this book wouldn't be here. Thank you for being my advocate through this process and seeing His timing with this message. Our journey is just getting started!

Allyson, Aren, Ayana, CC, Emma, Emma Mae, Georgia, Jordyn, Maddee, and Shelby, thank you each for sharing your story in these pages and believing in this message. God is going to use your stories in ways you wouldn't believe, even if you were told. It is a joy to call you all my friends!

Jennifer, Isabelle, Spencer, Rudy, Angie, Erynn, Victoria, Jack, Stephanie, Susan, and the David C Cook team, this book is out in the world because of the work you all are doing. Thank you for following God's lead and allowing me to be a part of this incredible mission. Your focus and obedience to Him are truly inspiring. I can't wait to see how God uses our partnership to bring Him glory and how these pages will help girls break free from what has been holding them back.

Julie, without your partnership, this message would not be what it is today. Thank you for seeing my vision and helping me shape what God placed on my heart. You have no idea how much of a blessing it was to work alongside you through the book-writing process.

Mimi, Papa, Nana, Hunter, Drew, and Tara, thank you for cheering me on always. I love you guys more than you know!

notes

Chapter 1: What If We Aren't Stuck?

1. Christine Caine, "The Power of Showing Up Right Where You Are," episode 186, *Christine Caine Equip and Empower Podcast*, MP3 audio, 3:45, https://christinecaine.com/content/episode-186-the-power-of-showing-up-right-where-you-are/gkmpxh?permcode=gkmpxh&site=true#.Y677rezMIbk.

2. Maria Konnikova, "Why We Need Answers," *New Yorker*, April 30, 2013, www.newyorker.com/tech/annals-of-technology/why-we-need-answers.

Chapter 2: When We're Questioning Why We Are Where We Are

1. Tony Evans, Twitter, September 29, 2017, 9:32 a.m., https://twitter.com/drtonyevans/status/913758308280004608?lang=en.

2. *Merriam-Webster's Online Dictionary*, s.v. "posture," accessed March 20, 2023, www.merriam-webster.com/dictionary/posture.

3. Walter A. Elwell, ed., *Baker's Evangelical Dictionary of Biblical Theology*, s.v. "heart," 1997, Bible Study Tools, accessed March 20, 2023, www.biblestudytools.com/dictionary/heart/.

Chapter 3: When Our Dreams Aren't What We Pictured

1. Lysa TerKeurst, *It's Not Supposed to Be This Way: Finding Unexpected Strength When Disappointments Leave You Shattered* (Nashville, TN: Nelson Books, 2018), 2.

2. Brigid Lynn and David Rock, "Exactly How to Adjust Your Expectations, According to Science," *Fast Company*, February 14, 2022, www.fastcompany.com/90721055/exactly-how-to-adjust-your-expectations-according-to-science.

3. Lynn and Rock, "Exactly How to Adjust," www.fastcompany.com /90721055/exactly-how-to-adjust-your-expectations-according-to-science.

4. David Rock, "(Not So Great) Expectations," *Psychology Today*, November 23, 2009, www.psychologytoday.com/us/blog/your-brain-at -work/200911/not-so-great-expectations.

5. Rock, "(Not So Great) Expectations," www.psychologytoday.com/us /blog/your-brain-at-work/200911/not-so-great-expectations.

6. "Dopamine Deficiency," Cleveland Clinic, March 23, 2022, https: //my.clevelandclinic.org/health/articles/22588-dopamine-deficiency.

7. Wayne Grudem, *Systematic Theology: An Introduction to Biblical Doctrine*, 2nd ed. (Grand Rapids, MI: Zondervan Academic, 2020).

Chapter 4: When Something Good Comes to an End

1. Live Original. "23 Quotes from Sadie Rob Huff," June 11, 2020. https://liveoriginal.com/23-quotes-from-sadie-rob-huff/.

2. "Hebrews," BibleProject, accessed March 21, 2023, https://bibleproject.com/explore/video/hebrews/.

Chapter 5: When You Don't Feel Loved or Good Enough

1. Bob Goff, *Live in Grace, Walk in Love: A 365-Day Journey* (Nashville, TN: Nelson Books, 2019), 128.

Chapter 6: When You Feel the Pressure to Figure Out Who You Are

1. Jackie Hill Perry, *Gay Girl, Good God: The Story of Who I Was and Who God Has Always Been* (Nashville, TN: B&H, 2018), 160.

2. James Clear, *Atomic Habits: An Easy and Proven Way to Build Good Habits and Break Bad Ones* (New York: Avery, 2018), 34–35.

Chapter 7: When You Catch Yourself Struggling with Comparison

1. "Beth Moore," AZquotes, accessed March 21, 2023, www.azquotes.com/quote/565489.

2. Brené Brown, *Atlas of the Heart: Mapping Meaningful Connection and the Language of Human Experience* (New York: Random House, 2021), 20.

3. Craig Groeschel, Twitter, January 12, 2021, 11:45 a.m., https://twitter.com/craiggroeschel/status/1349034655929016320?lang=en.

4. Alicia Nortje, "Social Comparison Theory and Twelve Real-Life Examples," PositivePsychology.com, April 29, 2020, https://positivepsychology.com/social-comparison/.

Chapter 8: When Your Life Feels Out of Control

1. Jennie Allen, *Nothing to Prove: Why We Can Stop Trying So Hard* (Colorado Springs: WaterBrook, 2017), 71.

Chapter 9: When You Are in a Season of Waiting

1. Paul David Tripp, *New Morning Mercies: A Daily Gospel Devotional* (Wheaton, IL: Crossway, 2014), 2.

2. *Merriam-Webster's Online Dictionary*, s.v. "wait," accessed March 21, 2023, www.merriam-webster.com/dictionary/wait.

Chapter 10: When You Are Called Out of Your Comfort Zone

1. David Platt, *Radical: Taking Back Your Faith from the American Dream* (Colorado Springs: Multnomah, 2010), 7.

Chapter 11: When You Can't Shake the Opinion or Approval of Others

1. Brené Brown, *The Gifts of Imperfection: Let Go of Who You Think You're Supposed to Be and Embrace Who You Are* (Center City, MN: Hazelden, 2010), 125.

Chapter 12: What If We Are Free from What Once Held Us Back?

1. Max Lucado, *Just Like Jesus: A Heart Like His*, 2nd ed. (Nashville, TN: Thomas Nelson, 2003), 125.